THE WEEPING GODS OF MANIPUR

The Crescent Highlands and the Dark Rainbows
Hijam Monarsingh Dallo Rihmo
Manipur

Dedicated to the people of the highlands, the mother, the children, the brave hearts and the many people who have lost their lives in the labyrinth of violence that has forever become the emblem of this beautiful country, the crescent highlands.

The book is a mix of quotes from books, some are stories passed down by elders, while others are experiences that shaped my opinion. Some of the writings are personal yearning, interpretations and understanding. While others are historical reflections as is in the list of books mentioned in the last page. The last section contains fictional stories depict post conflict Manipur. This book is a work of literature and it does not intend to incite violence, defame any entity, or promote separatism. All historical references are drawn from publicly available sources and folklore, with no intent to misrepresent facts or encourage unrest. Any resemblance to real-life incidents is purely coincidental. The author does not take responsibility for how readers interpret or use this content. Readers are encouraged to conduct their own research and consult official sources for historical accuracy. The works are at best, an expression of anguish and pain.

~*~

CONTENTS

Preface

I write this book to tell the other side of the story. The intention, to take you to various points in time, through poems, experience and also short writings on various aspects, offering you a view from my perspective and opinion, that may perhaps tell the story of the victims and their life. From foraging mushrooms in the hills to feed, to murders of the most evil, the narrative will be honest and in simple English' Someone has to tell the story of the common folk living through this nightmare we 'Manipuris' call life.

I imagine the victims are so many, it is enough to make a glorious temple of corpses. The book will attempt to present various stories that may perhaps shed light on the fast-eroding humanity or whatever is left of it. To be born here, the little moments of joy that sustains us amidst the sea of violence and killings, the tears, blood and indifference arising from too much violence, the normalization. Perhaps through my experiences and writings I might be able to tell the stories of so many like me who are unfortunately born here in Manipur. I write this simply because, if there was God, he has sinned, can he be forgiven, his sins they make the dark rainbows of Manipur.

Manipur is a hill state in the Northeastern part of India bordering Burma. The 'Native State' is home to tribals of different ethnicities of which the Meitei tribe is the most dominant. The crescent highlands which is also called the 'Burma Arc', is home to these tribals who essentially fit the definition of the 'Stateless Nations'. The territory of these tribals is arbitrarily cut in two, where one half is part of India while the other half is in Burma. It is also home to the longest running *liberation movements* in the world. The tribal societies here are traditionally 'communist' in nature – they are traditionally almost an egalitarian society.

~*~

MY NAME IS MANIPUR

My Name is Manipur
First, they came for my neighbors,
Roasted, burnt, bleeding,
Now they tell the story,
And it birthed tigers and lions,
Then they came for me,
Maimed, gagged, forced me naked,
Made me change habits and tongue,
Took my children to fight their war,
Took my brightest to crown their glory,
They wanted more and came for more,
Gave away my own like its theirs,
Stranger who come to rule,
Is it different from the seven years,
Is it different because it's no more swords
and spears,
Now they want the food from my plate,
And the riches from my land,
They want rivers of blood to scare,
They want my daughters for pleasure,
They lie that we are the same,
When I look in the mirror,
I see we are a race apart,
My name is Manipur,
It is no more the seven years,
My name is Manipur
It is but seven decades now.

HOW IT ALL BEGAN

The *Bloodless Revolution*, the telegram of 1949, *'Begins had discussions with H« H. (High Highness) of Manipur this morning H. H. threatens returning to Manipur without holding any discussion or signing agreement. H. H. must not under any circumstances be allowed to return to Manipur with his advisors and I have accordingly instructed police to be detained here his party if they attempt to return before signing of agreement. Please telegraph immediately repeat immediately authority for detention of H. H. and Advisors under Regulation or by whatever other means you consider might be appropriate. Have already warned sub-area to be prepared for any eventually in Manipur. Grateful for further instructions. Ends. Will keep you closely informed of further development (if) here addressed'*

Manipur Violence 2023, if history is anything, Delhi likely mishandled the ensuing 'anarchy' in the state again. Unfortunately, Manipur too has a history of it. There is a lot about the anomaly in the state too. At first, I thought this was just another clash, but it was unrelenting. I'll never know if Delhi wanted to deal the way it did, perhaps they have reasons, perhaps it is wise. But Manipur was drowning and it still is anyway. Elections are still going on in the country, it's sad how the other Northeastern states appear to be either helpless, or have they decided not to reacted at all to the development in Manipur. It breaks my heart.

The Marriage Of

'1919 & 1949'

Manipur, the birth of the FMR (Free Movement Regime). I feel the free movement regime was probably conceptualized to allow the tribes living on either side of the Indo-Myanmar border, the nation and its people torn in two, to move freely across the border owing to how unjustly the highlands have been divided into two. This is a most despicable way of treating a nation. I feel they only wanted the land and had no regard for the people who live here. Some of the passages I read talked of U Aung San being invited to come to the state of Manipur, this is around 1949. Nehru was aware of it, U Ba Choe replied that it will neither 'encourage nor discourage', this was to do with the merger of the highlands to either Burma or India. Culturally these highlands and its people share more affinity with the other tribes living in the highlands of Burma, further north however there are tribes that resemble or share affinity with the Tibetans. This brings us to the contested, 'Kabaw Valley', which was rather a curse for both Manipur and Burma. It, becoming a bone of contention between the two rooted in the 'Treaty of Yandaboo'. Here's what I've read about the 'Kabaw Valley', the valley every Manipuri feel is a part of their soul itself. This valley however much contested, Manipur only realized it along with the Pong King, never really able to keep it for too long anyway, the goings on I shall describe in the following passages.

The Shan state and Manipur will cross paths in earlier history. If one reads the Court Chronicles written by Nalini Parratt, they will find illustrious mention of Manipur as a full-fledged kingdom. True to it, the narration below compares some books, the readings mainly between 777 AD and roughly 1850 AD. Which may also put an end to the various confusing literature and sources that's perhaps aggravating the situation at home, religious, cultural, social and for Manipur – 'National'. A breakdown of the very idea of Manipur itself.

A glimpse of Manipur, the year is 777, the Shan Raja Samlong on his return from the invasion of Tripura kingdom, mentions two tribes of Manipur in particular, the Moirang and the Meitei. This event is mentioned in the court chronicles around 698 AD. The process of amalgamation of tribes haven't commenced as such. They were perhaps engaged in un-ending feuds like how the hills are till now. Manipur at this time is pretty under developed according to the sources, her tributes from various principalities to the Shan King while he was here, were politely declined. The passages seem to indicate the king found the tribute, too 'humble'. To the Moirangs, the king instead requested the tribute be offered to the Gods. *This will become the 'ritual' of the Moirangs in what I think is the annual pilgrimage to the 'Thang Ching' hills.* The Meities too offered tribute to the king, but he excused himself demanding from them that they only dress more decently. The passage goes on to tell that Manipuris around this time had the habit of masticating dried fish. A practice which was universal among all inhabitants of Manipur. In the chronicles, the narration gives one the perception of a glorious kingdom engaged in wars and with the neighboring chiefdoms, a well-established kingdom, the passage by Raja Samlong however throws light on the society and the actual state of affairs back then. Perhaps the route taken by him on his way home is what is the 'Pong Lambi' that we know. Perhaps it explains the various Shan influence in the culture and tradition of the Meiteis.

In 1475, with the establishment of the Meitei Supremacy, Chief Kiyamba comes into picture. By this time the Meitei chief is important enough to promise his daughter to the chief of Khambat. The daughter on her way to Khambat however, changes her mind and with her father's permission marries another – The Pong King (Shan). The Khambat Chief considers this an act of insult, war breaks out. The Meitei chief together with the Pong King becomes victorious and batters Khambat. Manipuri power rises and her territory expands to Khambat and Kale. The marriage of the princess will bestow 'Manipur' a spur of development. Manipur by now becomes a regional power.

Summarily, the notion that the Meiteis migrated from other parts is perhaps wrong. The most logical explanation being *descendants of the hill tribes*. The valley, through contact with the outside world advanced, and their culture and tradition influenced to such an extent it has become a civilization itself, a mixed race – *The Meiteis*. As far as records go, they had the Shan influence, the Mosuls, the Hindu, perhaps it is the very reason why we see a heavy cultural similarity with SE Asia and India, a syncretism.

In 1714, Pamheiba or Gharibneewaz, a 'Naga' by birth, adopted by Raja Charairongba (contested). In his reign Manipur will flourish with her territory going as far north as Kohima. To the east, the Chindwin, and to the West, the Cachar. The boundary to the south is never settled (This is also evident in other books when it was finally brought to a pass by way of an agreement with the Kukis – The Moirang Treaty).

Ghareebniwaz will later be murdered by his own son Chit Sai on the banks of the Ningthee (Chindwin) river in Burma. The passage goes to narrate that the son 'lusted' after one of his consort queen, and in doing so. He barred his father, re-entry into Manipur on his return from the failed expedition in Burma. The father appears to be an expansionist. In other books, it says he was 'decapitated' on the river banks along with his other son, Sham Sai.

The 'Moirang Treaty' is possibly the most significant in Manipuri history in relation to the Southern Tribes. If it exists, that is, the mention of this treaty is however doubtful in the sense, that it may merely be a Royal Order, perhaps an understanding? While its formal documentation is questioned oral tradition maintains its significance. But how does a king sign a treaty with his subjects, let alone Chiefs under his rule. In it, they say the Kukis who are kith and kins of the Lushais offers the Meitei King a stop to the incessant raids and pillage inflicted upon Manipur by the 'ungovernable' Southern tribes. This in exchange of a place to settle, and guns from the king so they protect themselves and the southern border. The Southern part of Manipur will then become the heart of an umbrella of so many small tribes that come to form the 'Kukis'. The Kukis being blood relatives of the Lushais effectively stop these raids. Ushering an era of relative peace from the almost annoying and unrelenting raids that 'necessitated' added a cost to the royal treasury. These raids fall in line with folklores from the other southern tribes that talk of unending cycle of violence. The boundary of the kingdom proper or reach under the Meitei King's direct rule in the south ending with the 'Loi' – marked by the abodes of the two southern wardens, The Thangching and the Wangbren. This will also perhaps explain why the 'Thangching' Is sacred to all tribes living close to the hill. Similar to the

'Wangbren' which is worshipped by tribes living close to the hill before the advent of Christianity. It will be noteworthy to mention here that the kingdom of Manipur extended even to the Lushai hills but it was never able to keep them under their rule for long, the southern tribes were rebellious and would never accept the authority of another. There is mention of a stone 'edict' in the Lushai hills that is perhaps already destroyed. Another one in 'Kohima' still survives.

The Court Chronicles of Manipur probably was written during Kiyamba's reign and re-written during Gharibneewaz's reign. As some of the sources and writings pointed out the 'passages' preceding his reign indeed are short and not worthy while the passages in his reign and after become more detailed. This would also mean Chit Sai, after ascending the throne, possibly rewrote the Court Chronicles and added the earlier versions preceding Gharibneewaz's reign. For example – *The Khuman Kangleirol*', was written during his reign. An attempt at tracing the genealogy of the Khuman Dynasty. It is in my opinion, a rewriting but necessary to suit the political needs of his time, to assimilate power and legitimacy.

To save confusion, I feel it's important to state that the hills were under the rule of the sovereign but indirectly. There is a whole book on it, 'Historical account of the Nativist of Manipur and hill territory under its rule 1873.' The many chiefdoms accepted the Meitei sovereign. The court chronicle is a tale of subjugation and also depicts many instances of chiefs who come to pay their respects or tribute. This brings us to the *'Kabaw Valley'*. If asked if it was part of Manipur the answer is yes, it was conquered. Of the ownership one must read the chronicles concerning King Marjit, the ownership becoming obscure henceforth culminating in the Treaty of Yandaboo, 1826.

The commissioner in Sylhet in his letter dated 19th April 1826, clearly indicates that the Ningthee, is the boundary between Manipur and Burma. A part of the letter to the Government of India;

'..unquestionably most desirable that the river Nlngthee (Chindwin) should form henceforward as it did of old, the boundary between Ava and Manipur, and Gambheer Singh having been in possession of Pergunnah Kubo when the treaty was signed we are fairly entitled to require the relinquishment of that integral and material of the King's Raj, still, however, if the point contested by the Burmese on the ground of the pergunnah having been formally annexed to the territories of Ava for some years prior to the war, whilst no provision is made by the treaty for any alteration in the existing boundaries of the Raj, the question must be settled by negotiation on the best terms that circumstances will permit."

Summarily, the error of the boundary lies with the Burmese, intentionally indicating a river flowing west of Ningthee as the river itself. The attempt to correct will continue for several years. In relation to the article 7 of the treaty, containing instructions to fix the boundary between the states of Manipur and Burma. The letter below to the Burmese ministries from the chief secretary to the government;

"..what places and territory in the ancient country of Manipur were in possession of Gumbheer Singh at the date of the signing of the Treaty of Yandaboo, the Governor General of British India considers it but just and proper that all these should still belong to that chief. When the British Officers in Manipur prove to the Burmese officers on the frontier by living witnesses and by undoubted testimony that so late as the years 1809-10 or 1811 the towns of Khambat, Woktong, Tummoo, Mungsa, and Sumjok comprising the whole of the Kubo Valley from Khambat, north, were held by Manipuri Thanahdars on the part of the Manipuri Rajah Cheroojeet Sing, the Governor General of British India trusts the King of Ava will perceive the propriety and advantage of putting an end to all further discussions on the subject."

9th Jan, 1834 – Manipur was granted 500 sicca rupees monthly as compensation for the loss of territory. In the final letter of the Government, dated 16th March 1833, that in the spirit of amity and goodwill between the two countries, the Supreme government cedes Kabaw Valley to Ava and the establishment of the boundary line at the foot of the Yoma Doung hills. The arrangement appears to be made to make governance easy on the part of the British and nothing to do with the rightful ownership. The payment of 6000 siccas were to cease in the case the territory was reverted back to Manipur. Then after, there's the letter, the 'Queen's Proclamation' dated 1st Nov, 1858, the British perhaps thought they would remain in India and perhaps the ceding of Kabaw Valley was a temporary measure. But later on, the siccas stopped, Manipur lost a part of her territory along with the people living there.

Now that we have a fair understanding of Manipur and the Kabaw Valley and why the FMR (Free Movement Regime), *let's move to 1949*. By this time Manipur already has a constitution, the Manipur State Constitution Act, 1947. But, in the 30th Annual Congress, there was a certain Tomal, who demanded the abolition of the 'Gaddi' and the Indian Union takeover Manipur immediately in line with Bordoloi's letter in which was clearly outlined the interest of India. It will seal the fate of Manipur. There are some familiar names in the high command they say, that may be of relevance in the Indian context.

'Pattabi Sitaramaya & Patel'

'Is there no Indian Brigadier?' — I understand that it meant, we are not very Indian to India – I can't help but feel like we are the expendable kind. Even now if they say we are Indians, very sadly their actions and

attitude tell otherwise. The Bloodless Revolution, I understand is nothing but a hallmark of 'dishonesty', a ploy, the rumor that his younger brother, Rajkumar Priyobrata will be installed as the Maharaja made the king jealous and he signed the accord - The Merger of Manipur, September 21, 1949.

When I read the history of the country, I can't help but feel like as if the education system is designed to completely omit the 'history' related to the Northeastern part of India intentionally. There was a time when we tell people from the mainland that I belong to Manipur, the first thing they'd ask was – 'Where is that?'.

The *'Shillong Accord'*, this I feel is no way to sign an agreement. I wonder, how does one even rule this way. It seeded the longest running insurgencies in the world – perhaps it has roots in the forced abductions, killings, rapes and burning of people, villages – the erasure of culture and indigene, perceived or real. No mention of it in any news or even books, because around this time the hills was a backward tract and no one would know what happened here. No one appear to care even now anyway. And when they retaliate, they are called anti-nationals and 'terror organizations' forgetting the atrocities they committed. I feel there's always the other side of the story. We became part of the country India, willingly or unwillingly. But the way it has been governed. How violence of 2023 went unchecked and it went on till the time of writing this nineteen months later. It makes me wonder; it is very unfortunate and sad what is happening here. My home Manipur is marred with such level of violence. The gates to 'The Kangla' is now forever a site of naked protest, our bazaars and neighborhoods, the site of fake encounters. The very place where I am writing this book, the small hillock to the west of Imphal, the Langol – a site of summary execution. The hills have their own stories too, it is no less horrifying, a genre of its own altogether. It's a chapter of inhumanity and evil of the highest order, mass rape in the hinterlands we will never know about, killings in hundreds that will never become news, the stories we only tell each other among ourselves. Perhaps all this have become fuel for further insurgency – I and so many other like me who look like me, dress like and talk like me, forced to live with it, spanning decades. Manipuris Lately, they are killing each other, made to see the difference between them when in fact they are the same people, speaking almost the same language. How does one stop such aggression and violence of the vilest kind;

The kind that makes the Gods shudder.

THE WEEPING GODS OF MANIPUR

If I were to die, don't burn me,
Give me a proper fire burial,
And my ashes, scatter them,
In the turbulent waters of Irang,
Or the snaking flows of Iril,
And in my second burial,
Take my remains to Sugnu,
The confluence of Chakpi and Imphal,
Make me a mound,
Bury me there on the banks,
So, the deities can see,
With their searching eyes,
From the hills of Chandel and Phiral,
Then, shall my soul in peace,
Make the coo-ing sounds,
Like the ones in stories,
Along with the spirits,
Forever becoming whispers,
Voices trapped in crystals and stones.
Among the hills and valleys,
Between the blind pine trees,
And their humming,
With no one to care,
Innocence so red,
It's beautiful and sacred,
And my cries, they become,
The shimmering tales of Manipur,
Along with the spirits,
From the hills I'll see,
My rape and desecration,
And along with the pine trees,

I'll hum when the winds they blow,
To forget and erase,
The pain and memories,
And when my eyes they can take no more,
I'll tell the blind pine trees my tales,
And gouge my own eyes,
To be together with them,
For it is too much,
For my little Manipuri heart and soul,
Silent and cold, the hills they watch,
And my tales, the God's they weep,
And from their hearts its springs,
Lilies and orchids.

Jiribam

East India Company and Manipur, the treaty of 1833. The ownership of Jiribam is contested at this point by chiefs who have perhaps declared themselves Rajas. In history, Maharaja Gambhir Singh, aided the British in the conquest of the – 'Khasi Hills.' Manipuri help was instrumental in subjugating the hills, this would also include the – 'Naga Hills & Lushai Hills', both places being the site of the stone edicts. The Kohima Stone survives, the Lushai Stone probably destroyed (I've only come across the drawings in books). This, though the conquest and rule were separate in the sense, the administration of the hills (Outside of Manipur's hill territory) was solely in the hands of the British. The Manipur Hills, were under the king's indirect rule. The treaty of 1833, the second such treaty between the Maharaja and the East India Company ceded Jiribam to the sovereign then. An instrument of perpetual ascension to the kingdom of Manipur. I don't think there is and there should be any contest as to; the ownership of Manipuri territory or its constituent hills or valleys or even Jiribam. If India inherits Manipur from the British Raj, it inherits the legal responsibility too.

(Aitchinson's Treaties, Engagements and Sanads).

Days before the hostage killings reported on the 19th Nov, 2024; like earlier, the state government decided to simply effect a blanket lockdown making life more miserable. No internet and a curfew in addition to the extension of the dreaded AFSPA, a draconian law at the center of everything 'Indian Atrocities'. Reading this from the local daily, *'The Sangai Express'*, it reminds me of how as a kid, I read the paper in shock about the news of half-mile tall twin towers in America that came under attack.

Earlier before the violence broke out again in Jiribam. Things appeared to be settling down finally. It seemed as though the government was making efforts to negotiate and bring about a dialogue. Then all hell broke loose. Like the pattern of the ethnic clash that has gripped the state of Manipur since, it would be killings and then retaliation. Jiribam was the first site outside of the valley where violence broke out starting with the 'beheading' of an elderly man. This time around, it was a woman, burnt beyond recognition, brain matter lying out in the courtyard, a nail driven in her thigh, legs and arms missing from the torso, it sent shockwaves. After that, some ten militants/village volunteers prepared to retaliate, they were gunned down by the security forces. I saw a video on social media of the alleged militants behind a house in Jiribam. The security forces were smashing something with a shovel, if rumors are to be believed it was likely the Hmar militants. This was followed by the news of the abduction and gruesome murder of six IDPs (Internally displaced people from the violence) from a relief camp.

The report;

'.... smashed the head of the infant and part of it is missing while the body of the two and a half year old boy was found with his head and arms missing. It went on to state that the head of the eight-year-old girl was also found smashed and the body showed suspected signs of multiple sexual assault. Bodies of the three women also showed signs of suspected sexual assault..'

In the contest of narrative, the civilians, we pay the ultimate price – almost usually, a heinous barbaric murder at the hands of militants. This renewed carnage follows the uninhibited murders and killings. The state government taking no action at all, starting from the onset of the violence since the 3rd of May 2023. Starting with a puzzling video of a women running for her life, the face not visible, possibly around Torbung Bangla crying out for help and calling all Meiteis in Manipur. I remember dismissing it, the video was deleted soon after I guess, there is no trace of it any longer. Earlier in the day what is ATSUM (All tribal students union Manipur), had called for a statewide rally in protest of Meitei's demand for Schedule Tribe status - it confers government benefits. Before the 3rd of May, there was undercurrents of deep hatred that was palpable on social media between the Kuki and Meiteis. This goes as far beyond as one year before perhaps, even before the violence broke out. Burning of forests offices in Churachandpur, and then the Outdoor Gym, which was to be inaugurated by the chief minister himself. Towards evening, 4th May, Imphal was burning in many locations. The horror was unimaginable and to add to it there was no police in sight nor the army, this despite the fact that Manipur is a highly militarized state. I remember there was this particular video about a woman being gang raped, this unverified rumor went viral, this would legitimize and unleash a new form of violence, 'rape'. To my horror I saw the video of one of the unfortunate girls too minutes before she was raped and murdered, the girl hands folded, praying for her life to a group of womenfolk. But they handed her to the mob. Some guys dragged her as she screamed and that was all of it. I still cannot come to terms with the video having two sisters and no brothers. Later, the photo of their bruised and lifeless bloodied bodies came out on social media. Close to around 70-80 *Manipuris* lost their lives on this day. By evening, the place I was staying was burning in every direction. Sounds of explosions everywhere, I felt true fear for the first time in my life. Soon after, I too went to Chandel with mum and stayed there to avoid the violence, since she was a Naga there was no surety, she wouldn't get killed. Just a few kilometers away, a mother was burnt alive in an ambulance with her injured son and her cousin or something. News came pouring in how settlements after settlements were obliterated. Then came Sugnu's turn and around ten in the evening towards the direction of Sugnu from Chandel, I could hear the faint thuds of explosions and faint flashes, the town was burning. Days after was filled with reports and unverified rumors about mass rape in Manipur University campus and such. The days after was followed by sporadic incidents of violence, Delhi was completely quiet until the video of two *Manipuri* woman paraded naked came out on social media, this was perhaps a few months later, a few seconds from the Prime Minister himself. And it ended there, except for visuals of unimaginable horror on and off social media, and local news channels, no national coverage. We, Manipuris were on our own.

Moreh and Jiribam connects the state of Manipur with the outside world. Moreh is already overrun by other groups now, Jiribam now is perhaps is the epicenter for this very reason. I remember my dad told us about my great-grandmother who would trade between Imphal and Jiribam during her early days and how with that money she constructed the 'Sungoi'. These two places control everything going in and out of Manipur. So is the Dimapur road, I understand that road was constructed with the local labour, how tables turn. Confined and trapped in this tiny valley of Imphal – it feels like Gaza.

There are many other events, but I'll leave that. The tale of Manipur from 2023-2024 is in any case a macabre tale that is widely publicized, it needs no retelling.

A Choir of Cries

29

If crying itself could cry,
It will beg with hands folded.
If struggling itself could struggle,
It will defy till the last wheezing breath.
If seeing itself could see,
It will stare into helpless eyes, wide open.
If fighting itself could fight,
It will batter broken bodies.
If lifeless itself could live,
It will swim, floating in rivers.
If desperation itself could despair,
It will be blank with hopelessness.
To accept our pitiful fate, still lose it all,
The overwhelming chorus, a choir of cries.
And in heaven we weep and weep,
Till the rains they fall and fall.

Let me proceed to take you through the socio-political history and the make-up of the Manipuri society that may perhaps shed light on the social ailments and issues that are otherwise not talked about or perhaps they've gotten so used to it they don't notice it anymore.

At the start of my writings, I wrote about the telegram in relation to the 'Shillong Accord'. I trust people and society of that time had their reasons why Manipur is what is today, a part of the *Union*. But sometimes I feel this was the basis of the whole divide – 'The forced merger'. It appears as though to avoid regrouping and reprisals because of the 'forced merger', I think the political divide was made intentionally because ideally in governance it makes no sense. I will never understand this and I cannot help but feel *The Union of India* has so inherited the method of governance formulated from or around 1919, and possibly along with it the reasons as was written by the British masters then.

The State

There appears a myriad of problems affecting the state. Let me take the liberty to state some of the problems I feel is most pressing.

With the prevailing political construct, we now have three sharp political divisions. Ethnocentrism, and along with it, a sort of land apartheid within the same people. Assuming Manipur to be an independent country, given the organization, it is like we have made for ourselves three divisions, that would report to a head, the head of the state. How then, will we organize ourselves from here now.

The question of feudalism. It creates an implied parallel power structure. A flawed one. The land under the feudal territory however is always 'up for grabs', like it is even from the immigrants who are fleeing the conflict in neighboring countries. I would have reformed the administrative setup and land reform but that's just wishful. And we continue to adopt and execute these failed policies. The need for the law to evolve and cater to Manipuri needs is becoming difficult to imagine. On the other hand, the hillmen do not even own *his* land. It sadly belongs to their feudal chiefs.

Manipuri commonfolk, be it Naga, Kuki or Meitei; have died in scores in both hills and valley in the many events in our history A series of bloody events, massacres and deaths and disappearances, turning calamities which is taking place even in 2023-24. This, it is a vicious cycle of violence the state of

Manipur has become synonymous with. The violence of 2023 even now appears funded, very well-funded the violence has not just sustained nineteen long months but seemed to have become more formidable. Earlier, I felt the violence will die down but it only seemed to grow larger. The fracturing of our own society - maybe it is our own organizations, our elites or our leaders, perhaps they are the reason that precipitated into;

the polarization of our society.

Perhaps then, we need a change, perhaps, we need a new order.

The *bridging of our cultural and political divide*; the sore need to connect with the mass. The apparent division between the people and the intellects, the scholars, the possible reformers. The need to bridge the divide. The almost impossible task of repairing the age old 'shared heritage'. Perhaps, we have learnt and need to probably adapt to changing reality. What has happened is history and to go back, will probably mean a repeat in a more devastating manner.

Chauvinism and herd mentality.

Humanity and our crying hearts; The '*State under Trauma*', very likely its true. We flinch at the slightest hurt, probably stems from our bloody past. I'm not sure how does one fix such a problem. I couldn't fix myself even. But maybe we should learn to see 'their' hurt and not just 'ours'. There is no empathy it is all ambition.

I can only tell;

It is only people like you who know 'you' – how we become a force to reckon. A collective will. An identity, a tribe, a nation perhaps. But about us, it's like many crying hearts coming together.

But what will so many crying hearts do anyway.

FOR YOU AND ME.

I'll never know if it was intentional, but they failed to protect us. I feel they never wanted to. If it was about the opium farms, the profiteers are not us. If the state has innumerable security forces, they protect only them and their friends. Without connections, without wealth, if there are *deaths* in the violence, it is only us, the poor who die. About us, we were only continuing our daily lives not knowing anything about the violence that was going to unfold;

It was never our fault.

Yet we suffer, yet we pay. And when we protest, we are beaten into submission. Every single day our voices become meek and meek. Until it becomes all silent.

Yet it is our house, that burns. Our lives that are destroyed. Yet it is only us, becoming poorer and being suffocated.

It was never us.

What horrible deaths, we die.
God has sinned, – his hands are bloody.

It was never us.

THE MANIPURI DREAM

'Raalpa' — That's what my grandpa, Thunghring Khumlo used to call me 'dearly' owing to my father, who was a Meitei. As a kid I didn't think much, but now that I'm old enough to understand. It made sense, all the history books, all the stories, it tells of one community that was engaged in 'wars' among all the ethnicities, they wielded immense power and established a dynasty going millennia. The very meaning of the word 'raalpa' is warrior. And the Anal-Pakan tribe inhabiting the southern hills and hinterlands, knew the Meiteis as 'Raalpa'. To the north the Kowpuis tell stories of Meiteis as the only ethnic community with an 'army', not just adept but vicious and deathly dangerous, subjugating every ethnic community in their vicinity.

I still wonder, why the tribals prefer to live atop the hills. Not good for farming, difficulty with almost everything you do and most importantly 'water'. Only when the Meitei power waned, settlements and towns started to spring in the foothills and the tiny river valley, or the foothills or the smaller river valleys like Saikul, Koupum or Chandel. Manipur, she needs to break the ethnocentric disease festering its hills that has perhaps made way into the valley too. It is simply, *'Manipur is not Manipur without her tribals.'* Even if she were to live without her tribals, none including her tribals will ever live the life they dream – the 'Manipuri Dream'.

History of the 'native' state and the developments surrounding Manipur, is perhaps the first thing we need to understand if we have to even arrive at a plausible or theoretical solution, as I have attempted at the beginning of my writings. Starting with the hills, the Kuki are a group of tribes from the Southern part of Manipur and Nagas they live to the North. This in a broader study will bring us to the Chins, Lushais, Kukis and Nagas. All this in relation to the land and people of Manipur and thereby the 'Polity'.

~*~
The Immortal Sparrow
Cowrie shells,
Bamboo Baskets,
Headhunting,
Salt Wells,

Tribal.

~*~

THE BLOOD-LETTING OF THE 'CHINRAM'

In support of the claim that Lushais are a cross between Burmans and Paite, I shall make mention in later passages about *'TlangKua.' The following passages are mostly referenced and written from the perspective of the British Raj and therefore I feel it needs further research.*

This finding from 1850. The Lushai at this time was under six chiefs, of whom one was acknowledged the supreme - Barmoolin, under whom is 300 regular Burmese warriors. Lord of 3000 houses. It appears a kingdom in the making. Given their recent migration from the East, which will lay the groundwork of the 'Great Gal';

The war of the East and West.

A precursor to the Great War between North and South that will result in Kukis migrating into Manipur. Both wars, the most vile and bloody. The tales in other books account how it took hours to behead their own kinsman. A war so savage it will drive the population from the heart of the hills towards the fringes. A tale of the most savage. It evoked in me a weird mix of horror and immense sympathy.

What of the people then.

THE GREAT EXODUS OF TEDIM, 1870

After the close of the *2nd Anglo Burmese War*, there was a political upheaval in the Chin hills, what is now Mizoram in India and Chin hills in Burma. There was concentration of power in what was 'East' and 'West' Zoram. The 'lesser' chiefs who refused the authority migrated towards the hills of South Manipur.

Peopling of the Thado in South Manipur late 1800. The Nwites moved in two groups, one party going North and settling down around Mwelpi the site of an old Thado village. And the other party migrating into Lushai Hills and settling down among the Lushais under the chief Poiboi. The Tornlongs or Nwites were visited in in 1892 by the Chin Hills Political officer, who also met several of the chiefs again whilst engaged on the demarcation of the Chin-Manipur boundary. An earlier 'event' took place in 1872, followed by this event in 1892-93 resulting in the surrender of over 80 villages and subsequent *administration* of the Chin Hills. By this time the hill-men known as the Kukis or Khongjais, live for greater part North of Chin Hill boundary line in the hill territory belonging to Manipur. There was a total of 6 Kuki villages in the Kanhow Jurisdiction.

THADO

'The present 'chief' of all the Thados is a young man named, 'Koodingmang'. The Changsels and Thlungums do not belong to the Thado race, but as the Thado say, of some ancient races, which were in existence before they arrived on the earth's surface. The Thlungums are distinct from the Changsels, and the Thados themselves are divided in to the greater clans of Thado, Singshol, Chongloi, Keepgen, Hangseen, Hankeep, from which again have sprung many other clans inferior in rank but numerous as themselves, such as Chungfoot, Telnok, Holtung, Mangvum, Vumtan. The mother of Koodingkai, the head of all the Shingshols was a Changsel and so was his wife. The mother of Koodingmang, the head of all the Thados or Khongjai is also a Changsel.'

It says that originally, they were not migratory, but have assumed this character lately since their expulsion from their *own hills*.

The story of migration is a human phenomenon one that is accelerated by either scarcity or violence. This is all, in what we call – *'The Pursuit of Happiness'*. It is only human.

CHINS

It appears the Bamars called the Zo people Chin from their very early contacts in the 11th or 12th century AD. When the Burmans moved down to the Irrawady and came to the Chindwin they discovered basket carrying people occupying the river valleys, hence they called the river 'Chindwin', valley of the baskets – *Lalthangliana, Mandalay University, Dept of Burmese History.*

Others, The Ningthee is what the Burmese call the Chindwin. 'Chin' of or denoting the Chin people, 'Dwin' meaning water. Chindwin – river of the Chin people. If we compare this with the other Tibeto-Burman language spoken here among the southern tribes, it would be 'Duh' in Anal-Pakan, Dui or Tui in Manipuri Kuki.

This piece of historical statement, if it's true, coincides with the Bamar invasion of Arakan Kingdom, there will

be numerous wars until the establishment of the
Burmese empire heralding the golden era with many
city states under its banner.

KUKI

Origin of the word Kuki: This basket carrying habit also
explains the corruption of the Persian word 'Kohki'
meaning highlanders, to the Bengali corruption –
'Kuki', and as a derogatory term owing to their habit
of carrying loads in a bamboo basket, 'coolies'. The
basket which is also commonly used in the hills of
Manipur – Naga, Kuki Meitei alive. Locally it is called
'Saam' in Meitei.

In order for us to understand the migration and
settlements, we may perhaps start with de-
recognizing the political borders we have created. In
the original understanding of stateless nations, the
vast tracts of hills and valleys are but one terrain all
the way up from what is now Arunachal till the end of
Arakan Range, creating what I will call the crescent
highlands. The heart of their homeland being in the
'fabled' Chinlung hills (*Hills of the cave of the Chins*).
There was at that time no borders. The extent of any
sovereign's territory was perhaps marked by either a
stone edict or understood by natural barriers or
frontiers.

For us to understand the identities, broadly most of
the Southern tribes come under the Kuki
Nomenclature. While the North of the valley, it is the
Naga Nomenclature. Within Manipur there is no true

division, but if we move to Nagaland and Mizoram or Chin Hills, you'd see true divisions. Both; *Exonyms*.

HMAR

Hmar people were so named by the Lushais because they live north of the Lushais. The Hmars are in fact very closely related to the tribes of Mizoram. While the Thados migrated from the East Zoram or Chin Hills mostly, the Hmars migrated from West Zoram or present-day Mizoram.

However, we must also take note that around this time the boundary to the south was really disturbed until the so called Moirang Treaty was agreed upon. This will result in the many Kuki settlements scattered in between tribes and the many hills in the highlands.

The cognates of these inter-related tribes had come to Manipur and Tripura sometime around 1600 AD. They were called Kukis (corruption of the Kohki) by the then *Bengal Sultanate*. By 1850, the Thado or Khongsai started to appear in parts of Cachar and Manipur. The British adopted the term Kuki for the Hmars and 'New Kuki' for the Thados indicating their later migration. All in all, they are the 'Zomi', meaning highlanders in their language.

ZOLUTI – SUBJUGATING THE CHINS

1871-72: The Lushai Expedition was a success and it resulted in the administration of the hills. The current discourse and the many publications appear to be selectively referenced, a propaganda that they were never subjugated forming the basis of 'Zalengam'. In the many accounts of the expedition there is graphic description of how the expedition was carried out. It even goes to the length to detail how and when and why the expedition was necessary. The expedition lists a number of villages, the hills looked like they were 'wearing' caps of flames, referring to the burning villages that arc usually perched on hilltops, a scorch earth tactic. One can only imagine the horror inflicted upon the tribes.

Zoluti is the Mizo name given to the abducted English girl, Mary Winchester. She, becoming a subject of wide discussion in Mizo academic. The girl, because of whom the Lushai Hills lost their sovereignty. Around this time there was only Chin and the subjugation meant both east and west Zoram had already lost their sovereignty. The creation of the state of Mizoram and Chin Hills is a much later development although by this time there was already political undercurrents.

This expedition is but just one of three that I have read. This now brings us to the *Manipuri Kuki Rebellion,* of which I will try to explain in the next chapters.

THE MANIPURI KUKI REBELLION

1917-1919

The epicenter is the *'Surkhua'* village. It will be burnt down to the last house. The aftermath resulted in the burning of;

- *86 villages out of 198 Thado villages down to the last house. A total of 970 guns were submitted to the British.*
- *18 Haka Chin villages were burnt. A total of 600 guns were submitted to the British.*

It appears there was a lull in the British punitive measures not because the British were scared but merely because of the World War 1 efforts. This appears to be the main motivation for the rebellion too – this apart from the French Labor. Macquoid & Keary or others, stated very clearly that the decision was delayed to the last moment, terming the rebellion an 'annoyance'. Following the administrative report, it didn't seem to have much impact on the administrative part, nor the local economy. The resistance or the rebellion ended in a devastating failure but it is still 'symbolic'. Something that runs deep in the blood of the people living in this part of the world.

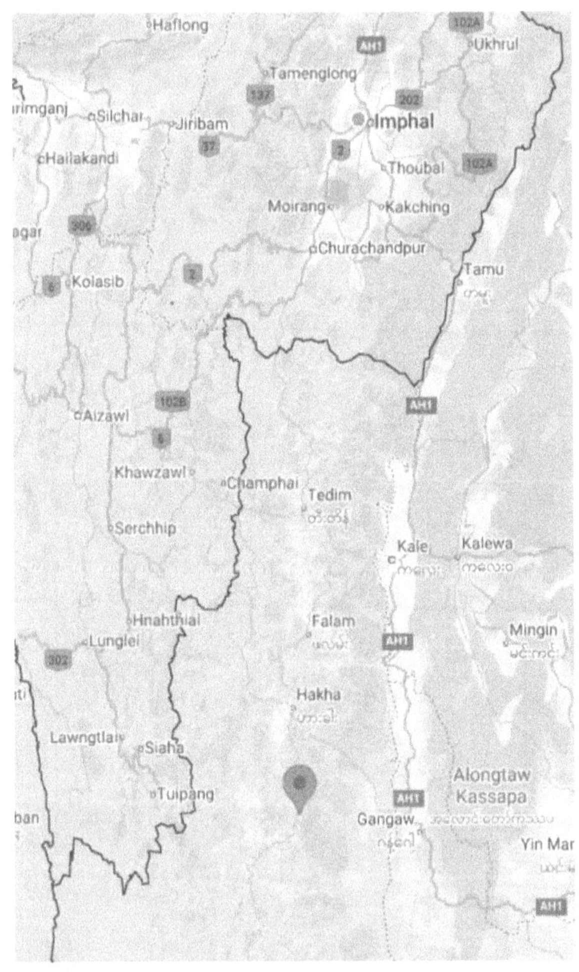

Surkhua town in what is now Chin Hills in Burma.

JPASB, XXIV, 1928

Fig. 1.—Chengjapo, Chief of Aishan, Head of the Dongngel clan.

Fig. 2.—Lhokhuimang commonly known by his nickname Pachei, Chief of Chobant, Head of the Hackip clan.

Fig. 3.—Khutinthang (or Khulkang), Chief of Jampi, and Head of the Shitlho clan.

PLATE 2

Fig. 1.—Enjakhup of Thenjol (the rebel leader)

Fig. 2.—Tintong, Chief of Laijang.

Fig. 3.—Suimang (commonly known as Pu-Silb) brother of the Chief of Kaujang; Shingdaun clan; wearing robal and thurpu.

JPASB, XXIV, 1928

PLATE 3

Manipur, 1929.

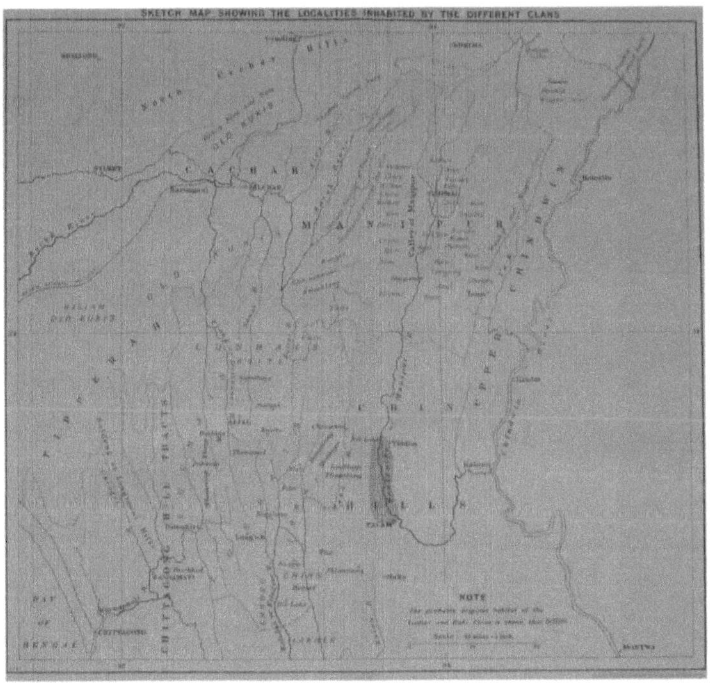

The Hillmen

The Guardians of Manipur. While the Cheitharol Kumpaba tell tales of subjugation, it's worth noting – the Meitei sovereign conducted these expeditions almost on a regular basis. In the words of the British, during the close of the First World War, at the summer capital, Shillong, around 1919 (Quelling the rebellion of 1917-1919), talking about Chingkhamba, Enjakhup and Ngulkhukai, they stated that the Meitei sovereign conducted, *'Periodical Massacres'*. It must be how empires worked back in those days even late into 1900s, village feud was common. This was perhaps, to keep the hills in check. But this, the three British officers were not going to allow it. In other books, the officers who were in charge, when the king requested direct control over the hill areas in later years, were swiftly rejected owing to the fact that the sovereign spent only one third of the revenue he collected from the hills. This we can relate in the understanding of the 371c of the Indian constitution and the creation of the Manipur Hills Autonomous District Council Acts. It will conjure a dual governance system.

Our story, the christening of the hills had commenced by this time. If it was *William Pettigrew* in the Northern Hills, it was *Ngulhao Thompson* in the Southern Hills of Manipur. A tribal who was part of the French Labor. The divisive politics is thus, *'properly'* defined from here. A separate 'Hill Administration' and a separate 'Valley Administration'. In the current context, there are similar sentiments in popular discourse, and there is no say that it will be limited to just one. In the event, the valley feels outraged, history is bound to repeat itself. The hill and valley share a morbid relation that is almost weirdly mutual, mired with bloodshed and blood bond obscure in myths and legends. But it is very clear that a strong hill country was its best defense. The hillmen by virtue of their position protected the valley proper 'with their life'. Even the Gods of the four corners (Guardians of the four directions) in the Meitei Pantheon appear to have wedded 'Tribal' deities. The hills are married to the valley. They simply cannot live separate.

Now that we have a fair idea of the people, land, events and its constituent history that helped shape the Manipur we know today, I shall write in the next chapters my experiences, sights, the colors and sounds that will form the basis of my understanding of the problem that ails this part of the region. And perhaps in the paragraphs, my thoughts and my un-pretentious brutal honesty, I might be able to offer an observation that is entirely unique and personal. A different view, while confident of the fact that you're aware of the limitations, if any, given the points that are important in shaping that opinion is made available.

There are certain inconsistencies, perhaps, in the court chronicles, which casts a doubt on other literary sources of Manipuri manuscripts. They have been re-written after the *seven years devastation* too. The bell metal coins in the museum, tell a tale that appears doubtful to me, the dates I have quoted 'selectively' in my writings. The establishment of the Meitei Supremacy in 1475 AD. The notion of 'one' accepted currency when there are different independent principalities is a little wanting. *But this all a personal opinion, maybe I have much to learn*. The other option is to barter or trade in weights. Therefore, I feel, the earliest credible numismatic sources of Manipuri origin must be no earlier than the 15th century. There are undercurrents of 'Supremacists' factors that's driving the divide in the Manipuri Society, hill or valley. Although, this is an entirely personal opinion and therefore I shall refrain from making any mention that may be at best a figment of my imagination. The manifestation of ideological foundations in both hill and valley societies however must be addressed if Manipur has to survive. We are a split society by now.

Humans, their ingenuity is a wonder. They learn very fast. They evolve. The studies of society itself is proof of this phenomenon.

Mankind himself is a work of art.

The next part of the chapter I will try to about historical references in together with the socio-communal settings. The devolution and reaching tentacles of the harrowing events that probably has helped in shaping the very complicated Manipuri Society we know today. In it, there will be instances of the political centers in the hill districts, a sense of deprivation and the injustice. How the various systems work in completing the cycle, although it is not explicitly mentioned it is implied. The almost crippling governance and the perspective of wandering Manipuri kid trying to make sense of it all with his little mind.

The Present

In the contest of narratives, we seem to have over relied on history. In modern day Manipur, maybe we should also remember our recent past and take a more holistic view of our past. In our many battles, in our nation building, it will be perhaps wrong to base on a certain period in time and discredit the sacrifice, the lives and effort that has gone in to make the state of Manipur we know today. And in it, perhaps the Manipuri Identity.

Making it all come un-done.

Perhaps, the victims did not deserve it at all. Perhaps they too share the same suffering like us. Perhaps, they too dream the;

'Manipuri Dream.'

The Dark Rainbows of Manipur

52

Manipur, is it you,
You sound so pained.
Let them help you,
Give them your hand.
Eat this fruit,
From the tree of liberty.
Tell the truth,
For the love of humanity.
Make your pain,
Your inspiration and strength.
Tell me while you can,
One voice, clear and sane,
Tell me what they did to you,
So, they know far and wide.
Tell the world what they did to you,
The dark rainbows and your plight.

~*~

In this chapter, I write whatever I can remember from memory that will perhaps give a hint of the socio-economic condition prevailing in the 'burning hills' around that time, between the many ethnic violence that has become synonymous with Manipur – It's hallmark.

1994 CHANDEL, EM SCHOOL, THE HEIGHT OF KUKI-NAGA CLASHES.

(From the memory of a child)

'A bright green praying mantis' – Being oblivious to the raging tribal feuds, it was the second time I'll be doing my KG1, that's what we call. I think the class was a terrible experience for her. There was a lot of crying and it was utter 'tribal kids' chaos. It's a different thing altogether. My younger sister looked up at me and said she wanted to pee. I took her to the corner of the class. A total disregard for the manner or toilet, whatever it meant back then. I too did my business in the same corner.

The school was mostly wooden and the woods were so old it had this greyish dark hue. Most of it in pretty bad shape. The walls of our class were what we call wattle and daub, rusting roof holding on to dear life. Our uniform was dark green then and many of us including myself never looked tidy. You couldn't expect much from a school located in Chandel in 1994 anyway.

2024 – I drove through the narrow streets along 'Panchai street' and saw the new school building at a slightly different location. A much better one, it is actually nice this one. This was next to the road. Nothing much has changed in Chandel anyway. Yes, the area where the school St. Peter's where I lost my silver chain still remained, the slope where I would slide down through the dust now all full of buildings and plants and trees.

Recently, Chandel population sort of exploded, it's curious how there are so many people and families now in a span of just 20-30 years. Many had shifted from near the Burma border and established new villages. I hear a lot of re-settlements took place owing to the Kuki-Naga clashes, I hear there was absolutely no help at all from the *'Government of Manipur'*. The people, they were on their own. No justice no law, just the hills, the victims, the people, the survivors. Many of them blood relatives perhaps. Their former villages and places forever abandoned and becoming someone else's. Most of them renamed and its existence obliterated. It was the way of life then perhaps.

A few kilometers away from Leikun, 8th MR, a new village would come up – 'The Paraolon', Lamkang tribe. All of them survivors escaping the harrowing bloodshed that was painting the hills of 'Chandel' – bright red. I remember my grandfather, Thunghring worked very honestly, in his own capacity he joined the meetings and perhaps assisted in the rehabilitation too. Perhaps the elders of 'Paraolon' still remember him. He would say they are our kith and kin.

Stories of blood curdling killings and horrifying narratives were rife around this time. 1994, perhaps was its peak. Comparing with 2023, it is pretty similar actually, just the number of deaths this time was much controlled but Government absence or inability is visible. Back then the killings were much brutal, it was mostly 'Daos' and a lot of cutting and beheading. Manipur Violence 2023, there is rehabilitation and assistance, 1993-1994 was a totally different story.

There was this famous story of two kids who travelled by bus alone together during the crisis not knowing where to get down nor where they are headed for. The story goes on to tell that they were perhaps siblings. I wonder if they survived the killings. I imagine it's unlikely given how even babies were not spared. Most of them were bludgeoned to death from what I heard.

'For all I know, the hills of Manipur is drunk with the blood of its own children. If the pine trees of Chandel had eyes, they would gouge their own eyes and prefer to stay blind, and hum every time the wind blows to distract themselves from the shrieking cries and bloody memories.'

These bright red haunting memories, I wonder if they have pushed the youths to pick up arms. If they did, who should we blame. The government or is it their fate being born here in a god forsaken place called Manipur, the playground of the devils.

About the Anal-Namfu, an early account of the British.
– 'At Hiroi Lamgang, a village at the South East corner
of the valley, we have a legend similar to that in vogue
among the Murrings, their neighbors, which presents
us with ancestor dwellings inside the earth. A feature
of the Thado Legend, and their horrible enemy who
devoured them as they emerged from the cavern. A
deity armed with two horns then slew the beast, thus
affording them safe exit from the cave, to which he
returned. The site of the cave in the hill called "Kang
Mang Ching", south of their present home. The people
of 'Anal-Namfu', a village close to Shuganu, also assert
that they came from the South and that they are the
sons of one of the two brothers and that from the
younger are descended the "Manipuris" (Meities).
They too took their origin from a cave on the slopes of
Haobiching. A similar place of origin is claimed by the
people of Sadu-Koireng. At Aimole, a small village on
the first ridge of the Hirok range, is preserved a legend
of their origin which declares them to have migrated
from the Takhel Lam (Tipperah Hills). The Thados are
among the earth born tribes and Dr. Brown quotes a
legend of the origin of the Angami Nagas much to the
same effect.'

Regarding the Anal-Namfu, the author is probably
referring to the legend of Khagemba &
Bungyangamba. These are legends or myths
preserved through folklores and tellings. The author of
the book and the hills tribes in the south were
speaking in 'Meitei' language even then. The 'Lingua
Franca'.

Kakyen

A mythical half bird half men creature. In Anal-Namfu (or Anal-Pakan) folklore, this creature (It is not very clear if it's half man half bird for the tribals but for the Meiteis this was similar to a harpy) finds mention, in the story men, women couldn't venture out because of fear of being eaten up. The creature was so fearsome. But one day a 'Petha' or hero finally defeats the creature. To commemorate the victory, they wear the feather on their head. In relation to the 'Petha', among the Anal-Pakan tribal polity, the chieftainship of the village or settlement is usually taken up by the hero the people choose. The one with who collects the highest number of enemy heads commands the highest respect. I'm told the front of the houses used to be decorated with the heads of the enemies, a practice which is preserved and now limited only to the heads of deers or other game from hunting.

264 CE, In the 'Court Chronicles' of the Meiteis, therein we find mention of the two brothers Taothingmang and Phunal Tenheipa, they travel south to 'Lokha Haokha', a village close to what is Shuganu now. There they kill the 'Kakyen' – similar to the dreaded creature that finds mention in Anal-Pakan folklore. The hero, 'Phunal Tenheipa', uses a 'Dule'. Anal-Pakan name for crossbow. We will find crossbows are traditionally used by the Anal-Pakan in Manipur, the other tribes preferring Daos or Spears.

Maanglen

Umang-wamangna maangba manglanla
Nungsibana Thumlaba Sanaleipak
Turelgi echelgi erei ethakta
Awaba lairaba singi marakta
Satlare ningthibi leirang Thambalna
Machu machu

Ningthiraba leikolna maangba maanglanla
Nungshibana Thumlaba Sanaleipak
Maphaam khuding jagoi esheitna thallaba
Awaba lairabasinggi marakta
Laigi sathek tamlare maikei maikei

~*~

Maanglen – stands for abode of dreams. The poem above questions whether these are the dreams of the forest (Umaang). It invokes the spirit of Manipur, the river currents, the people, how beautiful lotuses bloom in colors and colors in between the poor and suffering. In the second part, it talks of places and places soaked in dances and songs in celestial gardens, how in between the poor and desperate – Manipur weaves the movements of the Gods.

1996, PANGEI.

Pangei, Manipur Police Training School, restaurants were a new thing in Imphal then I guess, at least that's how I felt – We crossed the Pangei *Keithel*, and a little away on the other side of the road, we entered this hotel.

It was evening, no lights, we had to make do with lanterns and candles. Mum was not just disappointed but angry at my older sister for being so poor in studies. I remember she had this typical 'Meitei' problem with pronunciations. Mum was furious, my sister, she was almost in tears. – Fast forward now, who knew she will come up this far in academics. It's an envy. This despite all the problems we faced, the marginalization, the shunning, mainly from my father's family simply because my mother is a Naga – A 'Hao'. The term is now a disgusting derogatory word. Originally, the term Hao was applied to anyone who was not of royal birth. The king was addressed with the phrase;

'Nanai Hao Macha na'

etc..' meaning – *'Your servant who is an ordinary person.'* Hao meant a commoner; no subject spoke to the king in the first person but always in the third person. Sometime after the adoption of Hinduism by the Meiteis, Hao came to mean – 'Hill people' only.
The hotel, it had this benches and tables nothing much fancy. A young boy came to take the order. But something was wrong here there was general disgust

in the attitude. Something I will remember my entire life. This coming from small a boy and to a lady of the officer was quite daring I'd suppose. But here was a reason the boy had no qualms, simply because my mother is a Naga – a tribal.

There *was* utter disrespect for tribals in the Imphal valley. And perhaps, 'utter backwardness' in the Manipuri society, a contempt even within the same community perhaps. A general prejudice too against tribal women, how they are looked down upon and seen as less modest. My mother was visibly furious but didn't say anything. It was not for a *tribal woman* to protest. She simply does not have that right.

2024, even now there is no reconciliation. In fact, it seems to have gone so bad it is only, 'teething' now. Back then it was just us, no one cared. Now it's them too, and suddenly everyone is awake. – A social awakening since 2023, the Manipur violence. Even with wealth, it doesn't buy them respect in the Manipuri society. The social status appears to me by 'birth.'

A few tribes exercise this privilege or chauvinism in their area of dominance too. It means this problem is not limited to the valley alone.

It makes me wonder if all this is really in the past, or were we pretending. Perhaps we were.

1999, Churachandpur

A mind of its own.

We crossed Bishnupur, my dad will be posted here sometime later too. I will train and shoot a rifle the first time, scaring people in the vicinity. We went by bus my aunty and I, she my mother's older sister was married to a Singson descendant of chiefs — chiefs without land, every male born carrying the hope of one day establishing a *'Singson fiefdom.'* Their history, bloody and tragic, from a prosperous chiefdom to a narrow escape in the rains. I remember seeing small shrines, quite ancient belonging to the time when the king ruled over the lands, the Moirang bazaar, it was mostly rural, and then Churachandpur. The welcome was quite memorable, I would foolishly step into the mud, both feet a little above the ankle. I didn't realize it was going to be that deep

Bebe - My father was headed to a camp to negotiate talks and from the men guarding someone called out — 'Kapamo!' (First uncle). *My dad narrated* how he was shocked to see Uncle Singson's third son at the 'liberator' camp. Manipur was giving birth to a new 'armed group' around this time, just one of many. This one will become very relevant to the 'Manipur Violence 2023'. Getting posted in the hills, and I remember places like 'Maphou Dam', meant imminent death. I've never heard of my cousin then. The only last time I heard of him was his death. The story goes on to tell how he was given a 'Hero's burial'.

New Lamka, everything was almost wooden, except for a few buildings, the entirety of the town was sadly poor, just like the other hill districts but Churachandpur, it was distinctly not anymore Manipur. Here, even the Lingua Franca of the state, 'Meiteilon' was rather shunted, *Churachandpur had a mind of its own – a defiant one.* It didn't feel like Manipur. The roads were no road, most of the houses were shanties. The bazaar area was the only one that had some semblance of Manipur but for the people, a true definition of backwardness. And this sadly will shape my opinion about people from Churachandpur, prejudice.

Around this time, the town still held the position of the top district or town in India affected with HIV. She was the epicenter in India, I think Imphal acted too late, soon it will spread to the capital and many people will die of AIDs. My dad had the habit of playing the radio, I remember a radio announcement in 1996 at Pangei, the state government announced the discovery of this disease of which there was no cure.

2001, UKHRUL

I was at the house of one of the employees of Reader's digest, Ukhrul town. Uncle Henry would drive us there, I wonder if the office still stands. The office was a hut actually, mud and wood, lime plasters. Snaking roads, quite the dangerous drive owing to the roads. The roads back then was a pity. We would cross the village of 'Sikibung', it was famed to be a dangerous place back then. A village a little ahead of Litan. Then I saw the first Manipuri Tongkhul village, 'The Hundung'. It had an aura of its own, unlike the brick and stone buildings. Simply when you saw it, you knew you're in 'Naga Territory'.

Ukhrul has wooden quarters for the government employees. It really throws light on the 'Manipur Government's' efforts in the hills. Remnants of its former sky-blue paint or whatever survived of it, some windows missing, some with half the door already rotten and gone – ramshackle at best and the ones who occupied it were probably squatters. The government employees never stayed there they must have rent it out. It's a culture in Manipur. The employees earn extra income this way, almost all quarters apart from the ones in police battalions are rent-havens. I had the opportunity to stay at the house of distant relative, 'The Keishings', close to 6th Battalion Manipur Rifles.

I would come to Ukhrul in 2007 again, after my father's death to get some papers done. Finding a hotel was a nightmare, but we managed. Electricity was still a luxury then. I would spend the night at the hotel in candlelight. I had a hard time falling asleep not used to the darkness and the stark difference from Shillong life I got used to. The next day I would be meeting the 'Commanding Officer' of the battalion but rotten luck we only managed a 'Subedaar'. Getting posted in the hills even for a 'Commanding Officer' of a battalion at the height of 'Naga Ethnonationalism' presented its own challenges. It was in 2007, I saw the famed massive church in the middle of the town, the pride of Ukhrul.

NB: 'The Hundung' - I know that lately they have come up with new places with similar names. It's simply not in my memory. I might want to also make mention of the Wino Bazaar, a small stretch of wooden shops was the heart of its economy back then.

SPOKEN MEMORIES

Passed down from the elders of the hills. The covenants as told in oral tradition.

The first Covenant of the Umiam Lake.

'Angpu', would be the fourth born son. English education and manners to do the English work. But it would offer respite maybe. Life in the hills is so difficult. His name perhaps is still written on the walls of Union Christian College (UCC). He will attempt to bridge the Meiteis and the Southern tribes.

In his UCC days, the lake must have reminded him of the Naga ways, he took with him a *'mosquito net'* and indulged himself, doing what a Naga would – fishing in the waters of Umiam. A tiny cut perhaps from the rocks and he bled profusely. His blood, like

'Writings on the waters of Umiam'.

--

The second Covenant of the Umiam Lake.

The 'Keishings', they hail from the *Bungpa* mostly, a town near the Indo-Burma border. From the hilltop they say you can see the 'Kubo Valley', the vast plains and the extension of the highlands till the Yomadoung range and beyond, the 'Ningthee'. Here, let me pause and make mention of the literal meaning of the word 'Ningthee', it's a superlative adjective that is used to denote something of celestial beauty. The name, it bestows the river a title of profound beauty. The Burmese on the other hand call it an ordinary name, the river of the Chins – 'Chindwin'. Which itself tells us that the land beyond the Chindwin belongs to the Chins. The Chins in Burma are – The Meiteis, Nagas and Kukis. For Manipur, it is enough to know that it starts from Khamti in the North bounded by the river Ningthee in the East to the 'Namsuailuang' river in the South, a natural boundary, God gifted.

The descendants of the 'Keishings', would marry the same 'family name' written on the walls of the UCC. A blood bond, bridging the North and South – an entire conglomerate of tribes from the South will become part of the Naga Nation, thus.

--

The third Covenant of the Umiam Lake

In another parallel, Lake Umiam, she bore witness to it, quietly looking from its murky depths. The two boys they made the covenant.'

'The Covenant of Umiam Lake.'

Deep inside we all know this struggle; it is destined to be forever. Even if we were to submit, they will never see us as equal. If we signed even, it wouldn't last a generation. The new generations on both sides being born with visible differences;

'Forever a race apart.'

Since I have made mention of Ukhrul, let me add the following;

'THE WHISPERING TREES OF THE NAGA HILLS'

So, they ran, there was a crisis in the NSCN (National Socialist Council of Nagalim). A power struggle. He and a few odd comrades, numbering about seven. I can imagine they are almost out of breath. Barely breathing just inches away from death, it must have crossed his mind how of all the people. Who would have thought, it would be a 'Naga Women', who will save his life, she who will bring about;

— The dawn of the 'Isak-Muivah.'

Fast forward many years and now he is the face of the 'Naga Struggle', a forgotten path. A cause betrayed, people have such short memories. And so, the Naga Hills they watch silently and continue to whisper. Just like the 'Mekong', who so many thousands of miles away continue to cry. Memories forgotten. And the ones who die simply becoming;

— The Unlucky.

From generation to generation. It is the way of remembering in the hills. This is how the hills make memories.

Of the *second covenant*, I will try to write more on it in another chapter, the radio operator. And a glimpse of Irabot's leadership.

Angpu from the first covenant, his life will be short lived, just like Irabot. Their stories, they remain as whispers and whispers.

--

If I may compare an event here, and from the, '*Crying Mekong*'. The year is 1966.

'At approximately 5 in the morning of 18th November, the squad entered the tiny village of Cat Tuong, in the Phu My district, looking for a woman. After finding Phan Thi Mao (21), they bound her wrist with rope, gagged her, and took her on the mission. Later, after setting up camp in an abandoned hooch, four of the soldiers (excluding Storeby) took turns raping Mao. The following day, in the midst of a firefight with the Viet Cong, Thomas and Gervase became worried that the woman would be seen with the squad. Thomas took Mao into a bushy area, and although he stabbed her three times with his hunting knife, he failed to kill her. When she tried to flee, three of the soldiers chased after her. Thomas caught her and shot her in the head with his M16 rifle.'

This extract, it tells a story of heart wrenching violence that we are used to in Manipur. I wish to draw here the attention of the reader. The girl – 'Phan Thi Mao', although a Vietnamese look very much like our sisters. There's a commonality between people and races from the Northeastern part of India all the way till the Malay – we all look very similar; we all have had a share of a tragedy so profound. An un-intending party to violence and the stories that come out of these places, so hurtful, it can drive us mad. Some of the atrocities captured in photos are enshrined in the history of mankind to propagate the message of 'anti-war' of humanity. The very sentiment blossoming in the region itself, the very region in dire need of humanity.

Union Christian College, Umiam

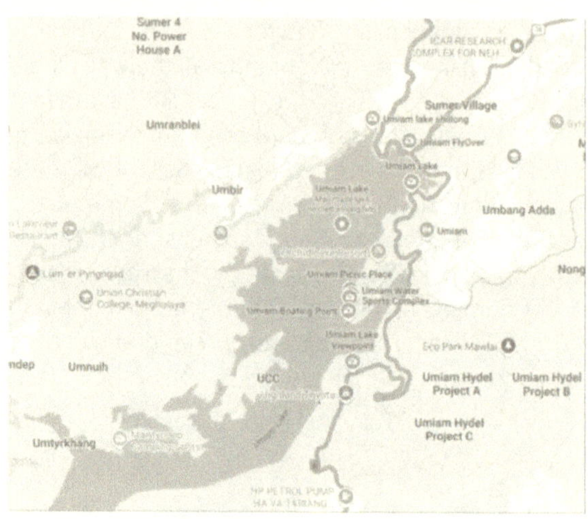

The Lake. Photo by Patricia Mukhim

Cold Memories

My father was finally resting; I imagine he must be in great agony every waking moment. Very kind of him, uncle *Elias* was always around, with the usual faint hint of tobacco. He gets it from 'Iewduh (*Bara Bazar*).' I think, he probably smokes pipe, although I've never seen him smoke one. Weather in town is very moody indeed, you'd have sunshine and then rain, warm and then cold. From the windows along the hallway, you could see Lady Hydari's park. Quite inviting I should say. How gloomy it was, I didn't know what to do. I miss him and I'm sure my mum does too. - I remember how I felt like taking a walk, the sounds of birds and insects and children playing. From a distance you could hear the creaking rusty sound of swings. I could see benches around the park. Manicured lawns dotted with trees here and there. Very peaceful to look at. I'd later read about *Lady Hydari* in books and history. By the time I write this book, I have read plenty already.

It was maddening, hazy, many of his trainees and his seniors from the Academy were all there. Uncle Syiem, Uncle Thangboi, Uncle Pachaua - I'd later meet him in his office at Imphal town. They are all unrelated, it was only out of respect I'd address them as uncle. Quiet boy, that I was and sometimes nervous. I didn't speak at all, he gave me this look, a little playful for someone of his station. When there's a family tragedy, I wouldn't know how to handle it. I simply didn't cry at all. Only trying to understand the things happening around me. Hardly any place to walk around, there was men in uniform everywhere. It was overwhelming. From the hospital, we took my father to the academy in a coffin. How my mother cried, I can still hear it in my head, it really breaks a son's heart. Uncle Livingstone was to accompany us till Imphal. The papers were arranged from the Commissioner. And we started our journey. I looked out the window as we moved, a long line of future officers of the northeastern states saluting all the way. It was quite a sight of brave young hearts. Future champions and heroes. We were finally on our way to Imphal, my dad finally in peace in a coffin Uncle Syiem managed to arrange from the Don Bosco. It was also my Alma mater. How everything is so connected. How do men with weak hearts endure.

--

It was biting cold; I saw the lake and was confused if that was the Ward's Lake they talk about. I have a curious mind and I checked the maps and everything about the place when my dad told me we would be staying in Shillong now. I was very excited.

We didn't have to wait long, he along with the driver was already waiting to greet us. The Indian driver in impeccable uniform shiny and proper in stark contrast to the uniform men in Manipur, and he with blazers and matching shoes, our first meeting with a *'Khasi.'* I'd later learn that men usually wore blazers here, it was a rarity back home. It was a change of scenery and coming from Imphal seeing someone in blazers really made an impression in my young mind. I was thirteen probably at that time and he was almost as tall as me. The driver was very attentive and spoke in a thick voice, he on the other had had a charming demeanor and was always cheery. When I think about him, I'm very thankful, he's probably witnessed a lot of my father's life at Shillong. Dearer to us than our own family. He would be there when my dad breathes his last at Civil Hospital, Shillong.

They said they shall honor him a burial at the cantonment. My dad's family refused. We went with his lifeless body in a very un-ceremonial manner.

As we moved, I looked at *Umiam Lake* with a heavy heart.

I will watch his cremation at Tera.

Imphal.

Lady Hydari Park, Shillong. Photo from the internet.

WANGOUPA LON

As you try to piece the bones asunder,
If your memory of decades is without
blunder.

Can you tell of that moment in the hills,
The hills of Wangoupa, where men speak
lilies.

Did you drink the water of Dutari,
The life and memory of Dutari.

Can you tell of that moment in the hills,
Where men speak lilies,
And weave memory of needles.

Can you sing in the voices of Dutari,
Sing the memories to Chakpi,
Sing in the voices of Dutari.

***

(Wangoupa Lon – translated is 'The hills of Wangoupa')
Located in the hills of Chandel

THE MEITEI ROOTS (IMAGINED)

If Sikhism is the bridge between Hindu and Islam. Then Manipuri, it would seem, is a bridge between the dominant cultures, the Indian and the Asian. An amalgamation of so many influences that shapes the mesmerizing culture we know today. Tribal by looks, Hindu by religion, Asian by culture, Hill-men by spirit – it seems as though it is a new born civilization, the one we so fondly call – *The Manipuri*.

In the Manipuri, there is the Shan element, the Burmese, the Hindu influence, the Mosul and predominantly the 'Tribals.' It is in fact, the tapestry of the people that actually makes the capital – Imphal. In her new found identity, she however, seems to forget that *her immediate ancestors are the hill people* – Their forefathers. Lost in her brand-new identity, she sees herself different. When in fact in her veins, the blood of her ancestors from the hills, they run thick.

Birth of the Lushai (1824): Descendants of Thangura (Union of Burman and Paite).

TLANGKUA, *North of Falam*: This is fairly recent, it is said a horde of Burmese army disappeared into the hills West of the Chindwin and never returned. The cross between Kukis and Burmese becoming the Lushais. And unlike their forefathers, they would make permanent settlements and gradually migrate westwards from *Chin Hills to Lushai Hills.* They would settle with the tribes and establish a new power center that will, like the Manipuri, conduct regular massacres driving smaller tribes in all directions. Not just the 'Kukis', but other tribes who refused their *authority* were forced out too from the *heart of the hills* spreading all across the foothills of the ranges and the fringes. Starting a trend of displacement and migrations and savage killings like an infection spreading across the highlands. The regular raids in the plains and kingdoms around will become a regular occurrence, it becoming more frequent than the last. The 'Great Exodus of Tiddim' and later migrations and events like 'The Great War of the North & South', 'The War of the East & West' would follow. These migrations will spread as far as Tipra and Chittagong and onto the plains of the river valleys of Feni, Imphal and Berhampooter. Supported by the fact how *'Khawls', Vaipheis (Compare fountain of the Vaipheis near Aijal)* and other old tribes of the Lushai hills now spread from Manipur to CHT (Chittagong Hill Tracts) towards the fringes of the thickets, earlier they were recorded to be living in the heart of what is now the center of the Lushai Hills (*A similar event occurred in the East Zoram or Chin hills*). Their appearance will be recorded in the chronicles of these sovereigns, as a savage menace to their kingdom – *ungovernable.* Their nomadic nature it appears to be mainly driven by some sort of self-inflicted, inter tribe, inter community carnage and the fertility of their cursed soil itself. Village of the same tribe indulged in killings simply owing to a girl's chaff or a wife's anger. It appears they only needed the least possible excuse to draw blood. The *Piler Hill* or the *Tuali girl*, fever or disease for that matter. No one village could settle permanently owing to the series of unfortunate and avoidable violence they would inflict upon themselves. It makes me wonder what of the common people under the chief, when the chiefs themselves are a *'favourite target.'* Their severed heads, commanding more respect. The obeisance and the selection of *'heros'* is also evident in the 'Old Kuki' tribes – what is called the *'Petha'*, and he would command respect from not just his village but if he proves himself – the entire tribe and the many villages thereof. Often times the chiefs were so brutal themselves, that their death was not regretted by their followers.

In this, the thesis of *'Terrorism and Terrain'*, *(Univ of Kentucky, also compare with Mindanao in Phillipines)* holds true. Slavery and human trafficking will become common in the southern highlands (East and West Zoram). The tribes would conduct *'terror'* and then retreat in to the thick of the forest. The captured 'children' from these raids that were brought to the Lushai Hills, will be subjected to slavery and they becoming docile, will live this way getting used to it. Human trafficking then became a flourishing business, with *2 muskets (American flint musket, G Alton) for 4 ½ feet high human*. The 'Poee' people would exchange the muskets for slaves (Govind Ram, Bengali interpreter). This firepower will aid the new found power-centers in establishing a strong foothold through massacres numbering close to 100 every instance, followed by a bloody, arduous and long hours of beheadings. This perhaps to instill fear and drive migrations, it's not very clear. The Hmars being one of the tribes that were displaced from the Lushai Hills. Becoming the Northern people or 'Hmar' to the Lushais and their settlement, *'The Hmar-Laam'*.

DESCENDANTS OF THE HILL TRIBES

The Meiteis, it would appear (the amalgamation, & different from Khuman, Moirang or Luwang) are a product of the Shans, and many other 'people' who came across the valley. Possibly settling and establishing the kingdom of Manipur with its center at Modern day Imphal. The Meiteis will amalgamate all other chiefdoms in the valley and bring about a uniform language and culture, each clan perhaps contributing an element in the tradition we know today. This is something the 'Lushai Hills' is doing in present day Mizoram even now, an imposition of cultural, linguistic, religious uniformity (*Read Mizoram's peace and Manipur's Mayhem, Hassan – London*). The 'Manipur Valley; unlike the hills is an open space in the midst of the hills and if history is anything, anytime the valley was in danger or under attack, the population would seek shelter in the hills. This happened even in the Anglo – Manipuri war (Read

Manipuri, not just Meitei), also during the 7 years devastation where in the valley of Manipur underwent massive 'de-population'. Many of its inhabitants fleeing westward as far as Sylhet. Just like how the current crisis in Manipur is also driving hordes of its affluent population. Manipur appears to be experiencing this symptom from time to time. The crisis now however, resulting in massive economic repercussions – the negation of wealth. The sad history of this kingdom being, their kings without an iota of heroism, always the first – to flee, also the first to return only to – claim authority. A similar pattern in the current imbroglio too, disappearing at the peak of *unrest* and suddenly appearing during a spell of relative calm.

The chronicles it would appear, when it was re-written, it added the names of the earlier chiefs as a long line of Kings of a kingdom. When in fact they appear to be, a long line of chiefs of independent chiefdoms, who by virtue of the assimilation already achieved during the time of its writing, erroneously (or perhaps intentional) recorded all chiefs of different chiefdoms as a continual line of succession under one 'umbrella' – The Meiteis. The reality being – the pattern of how each chiefdom in the hills were still warring with another even in 20th century Manipur, a remnant of its past. Sometimes instigated by the king at Kangla now, arming one to attack another, while at times conducting periodical massacres himself. This would also explain why the capital in certain years, was recorded to be 'Keke Moirang' This fact, is also supported by how the 'Revivalist' centers in Imphal now, confirms that there was many 'Kanglas' in the past. Indicating the capital or chiefdoms of each principality. This also tells us the valley of Manipur was a marshy swamp grassland earlier with parts of the higher ground appearing as habitable dry land (The Kanglas).

If the Meiteis were to look for their ancestors, it is the hill people from whom they have descended. Their new identity so unique due to the intermingling of different races, they have inadvertently become a new 'breed' of highland people. The younger generations without 'memory' or affinity to its past heritage. Tribal but unable to come to terms with it – a cognitive dissonance perhaps. Afterall, the valley is the heart and therein, everyone converges. Resulting in assimilation in her more modern civilized nature. From savage conquest and amalgamation to cultural domination and assimilation, and with it the birth of new surnames within the Meitei Society, losing its old self and reborn into the Meitei fold.

Therefore, there appears, no pure blood Meitei. The Meitei itself is a mixed race of which the tribals in the hills are perhaps the most that contributed to the mix (Inter community marriages and inter-tribal marriages). While the occasional dominance of other advanced cultures resulted in the paradigm shift – religion, architecture, rituals, food – all this, while maintaining a bit of her former self. In the making of the Meitei Culture; this – the supremacy of the 'True' Meitei culture is nothing but based on imagination that perhaps has its foundation on only a section of her history – a mistake. The story of Kangla itself is of one, wherein, the King moved from this traditional residence of a *'Naga House'* into the more Shan-like residence. Its inhabitants later imitating the courtyard-architecture of the Sungoi-Shumang-Yumjao, just like the Shans. From the Ahoms, from wooden houses to the *'wattle and doab.'* The similarities all too telling.

~*~

FROM FOLKLORES "MOIRANG KANGLEIROL" - MIGRATION FROM HILLS TO VALLEYS

Just a theory, but the notion of khunthak and khunkha, may have played a role in hill to valley migration. This is documented in Moirang Kangleirol. This practice is still prevalent in hill districts, where the people live on the hill tops while the farms are usually at the foothills. This was probably because of wild animals like tigers and elephants - still documented in Cheitharol Kumpaba, the killing of which was given a wealth of prize sometimes a lifetime's worth of Salt biscuits (Thum - salt was a form of currency back then). The early oral folklores of Anal Naga talk of such practice, where invading tribes would kill the people guarding the fields at night slowly decimating their population.

In recent times, Senapati town which is now one whole town earlier had this distinction. The khunkha will be closer to water bodies and naturally serve as farmlands. If Imphal valley was a swampy marsh. It's plausible, that the various tribes had these distinct tribal settlements. Which may also explain why the native inhabitants of Manipur are traditionally settled and practice agriculture. The valley being home to a variety of native rice grains perhaps will help in this theory. Over time, invasions and exchange may have facilitated in a new language or the language of the dominant tribe became more prominent - as is, the state is home to a group of languages that share some element of similarity and follow a similar syntax and structure. The Meitei language in essence still follow a mix of all the tribal dialects surrounding the valley. The most discernible being the 'Pa' and 'Pi'.

The names, Tangkhu and Tanghal — sound like Anal names and given how Moirang is close to it it's a possibility. The Chandel hills is probably what is the Laiching Hills. And if settlement pattern is anything in Manipur, the organic pattern of settlement is a long line of houses next to the river banks. The rivers themselves serving as means of transport even in late 50s.

THE TRUTH

In the history of modern governments, there are various political organizations that have competing ideas but all of them profess the same goal. By now, the earlier chapters I trust have equipped us with enough knowledge about certain peculiarities, that make up a part of the foundation of the polity of Manipur. From democratic to outright extremism. We can now perhaps theorize as to how to curb the problem. If it makes you wonder, why have I resolved to write such a book. I do so in the hope to start a chain of thought that will counter these issues while trying to address the various problems because now 'civilians' are being affected and this has become normalized. To sum it up, our bodies have started to become their battlefield.

Ningtam Laan

What is liberty,
Without Manipuris.
What is liberty,
Without the people.
What is liberty,
Without life.
What is liberty,
To the dead.
What is liberty,
When you're alone.
Tell me Manipur,
What is liberty.

A CALL FOR UNITY, THE LIBERATORS

Manipur is home to various liberator groups; it makes no sense in denying the truth. The liberators, they are a 'political problem'. The *Naga Liberation Movement* started from a political issue, so is the *Meitei Liberation Movement* – Earlier the government of Manipur did the right thing including these dissenting voices in the decision-making fold until the 'Pungdongbam Incident.' Herein, lies the root cause and the call for a separate country. The emotion of Manipur even now, despite the many literatures that brands the leader a communist. He is celebrated. Earlier when he was part of the political order, Manipur started to see changes in the society, these changes they cement his name in the foundation of the state and her people. More than a communist he was a social reformer. Also, if he took the communist political group for support, it may simply be because he did not have the support of the other political order, but that's a personal opinion given how the communist leaders were the first to sort of wholly support him, his life story and his interactions and inspiration. Here, I must make mention that communism can be understood in different context – for the sake of my deliberation here, I'll class them into Liberal and Orthodox. In reading the short paragraph you may have sense and perhaps wonder if including these voices that have become so extreme can be included in the decision-making body. And if you did, that is, then you and I we are thinking the same. A way of handling the core problem attached to the many movements it has given birth to. But before we make any arrangement. There may be pre-requisites. The fundamental answer to these movements should be understood first. If it is independence that they want – the question should be, why has such a demand come to the fore and perhaps solutions should be formulated along these lines. Independent or not – the end result is them at the helm of authority – but as an organization resulting from the people's legitimate sentiments. For anyone who even casually follows a bit of the history of the land and politics, they will understand that independence with these divisions and divided organizations will mean bloodshed and instability in the region bordering India and Myanmar. Perhaps a perpetual conflict and perhaps this was what the then premiere of Assam, Bordoloi saw and recommended the merger of Manipur. Manipur has always been the site of 'power struggle' – this, in the past as well. Her people becoming the victim in the process. Unifying these organization, is a dangerous *political gamble*, but personally, I don't see any other way. Or perhaps an alliance between them. This will give better control and a central authority of the valley-based liberator groups to deal with, in a democratic manner. There is no reason for them not to unite. Given the platform, they should become the political group that they are in honesty.

A proper understanding of 'insurgencies' anywhere in the world will eventually point to the source – the people. It starts from the people. If the people rebel, it is a sentiment and these sentiments they form ideas and these ideas they sustain insurgency movements. Without the support of the public, these movements become a mere law and order problem. If Manipur's insurgency has gone on for many decades, they seem to have only emboldened their resolve. Perhaps the governance is just not doing things right. And if the aspirations of the Manipuri are anything, perhaps the sentiment and their movement is also legitimate.

When the organizations they unite and operate as one, then the government can initiate negotiations. There is however, the problem of the 'political gamble' I have mentioned earlier – The ultimate unification of the highlands. The unification of the highlands too become possible then. But there is the government, and how do governments manage the emotions of the public is a different thing altogether.

Perhaps, the remedy to the insurgencies lies with the public itself. Without the support of the public, it wouldn't sustain. And herein, lies the issue of AFSPA as well (Armed forces special powers act). It will perhaps never solve the insurgency affecting this land, it may perhaps solve the law-and-order problem. To apply AFSPA in insurgency affected region will only give the people more reason to rebel and it will result in a stronger movement and perhaps a more violent insurgency. The liberators are also children of Manipur and when one dies a family in Manipur cries and with it the sentiments of the people are affected, it gives the movement a solid impetus. There is the government too, without the public's support governments, they fail, be it a monarchy or even a democracy. Perhaps it is all about governance. India had 75 years to prove their democracy to this region, perhaps it is time for the liberators (discounting armed gangs and other illegitimate groups that hide under the cover of insurgency) too, prove themselves in a *'democratic manner'*. There is however the conflict economy and the various organizations that may have co-opted and obscuring who is who, who are really with the people and who is not.

I AM A MANIPURI

I am a Manipuri,
With a grieving heart.

I am a Manipuri,
With an aching heart.

I am a Manipuri,
With a painful heart.

I am a Manipuri,
With a raging heart.

~*~

THE CRIES OF BOLJANG

91

The next day in the morning; I saw little kids with their schoolbags running for their lives. Some were crying, the oldest among them was quietly leading them away behind the houses towards the fields. Trying to tell the other little kids not to make any noise not even a cry. I'll never know where they were headed. I decided in my mind that we too had to leave.

In another place, I saw people fleeing for their *life*, it felt as if violence was following me. He said he was the son of the Boljang chief.

I'll only mention here the piercing cry still fresh in my memory. His cries they echoed and echoed. The pain they were so deep;

very deep.

Yet again,

In another time, I saw people fleeing for their *life*. Manipur was going to witness an unprecedented scale of violence. It was inevitable, the senses they simply knew, this tragedy that was going to unfold. It had already begun;

In colors and colors.

3RD MAY 2023

Before I make any mention of the violence, in order to get a complete picture. It is important to understand the Schedule Tribe demand. This in my earlier writings is already clear why certain sections latched onto this demand, a new organization Schedule Tribe Demand Committee (STDCM) was set up in Nov, 2012. The immediate problem on May 3rd 2023, was the counter blockade or counter rally. The police did not provide protection to the people conducting the rally, which likely resulted in the violence. We must understand the fact here that, the hills can 'never' organize a rally in the valley districts. Similarly, the valley can 'never' organize a rally in the hills. It has never happened in the history of Manipur nor will it ever happen in the future as well. The hill districts now have resorted to highway menace (extortions) affecting the entire state. The Meiteis however being in the capital when they announce a shutdown of the capital it affected the hill districts immensely.

Communal or Democratic Civil Society Organizations

Manipur And Its Hardening Communal Electorates.

'A civil society organization (CSO) or non-governmental organization (NGO) is any non-profit, voluntary citizens' group which is organized on a local, national or international level.' – United Nations.

'An organization that takes decisions and enacts laws on behalf of a country's population is called a government. In this article, we will talk about what government is, its types, levels, and functions.' – In short it is an organization.

I should not go into the details of a definition and structure like an academician would. I cannot force myself to sit and read voluminous papers. I will instead, to the best of my knowledge, simply write about the CSOs in Manipur and how it appears to function, the way I see it. The definitions I hope prepares the groundwork for the story I will write below.

This will be around September 2023. It would have never interested anyone In the workings of grassroot unions and assemblies. But perhaps it chanced, and I enquired about the absence of tribals in AMSU (All Manipuri Student's Union). Perhaps there are, but as far as memory goes decades even, the office bearers or the names of the leaders appear to me all 'Meitei.' It appears the three groups have made for themselves their own unions, often competing. But outside the state of Manipur more amicable, the phenomenon weirdly only in the state itself. An academician would perhaps call it 'dangerous', I think it is too. I feel it feeds Ethnonationalism, and instead of 'mediating' they best become anti-government, anti-community, a fracture. If a tribal body raises an issue, the other group would organize a counter. This will take us to the *'Tribal Solidarity March'* of 3rd May, 2023. When the hills organized a rally, there was a counter rally in the valley and where the boundary of the Meitei Land and Tribal Land is believed to be, the violence broke out. This appears to me the true epicenter of the violence, it was perhaps, never Churachandpur. These ethnic divides from the grassroot level probably resulted in the deathly divide that seems to have only hardened even after the violence of 3rd May 2023.

It is simply not possible and unthinkable for the Meitei CSOs to carry out a protest in the hills, likewise it is impossible for the tribals to carry out a protest in the valley. This is perhaps where the Meitei groups assert their historical claim to the land. This then developed into a full contest of narratives based on history and who were the later migrants and who have descended from whom.

In context to the topic of discussion, if there is AMSU, the tribals have made for themselves the ATSUM (All Tribals Students Union Manipur), the organization that spearheaded the Tribal Solidarity March. The ATSUM executives apparently were mostly Kukis and it is believed the decision was not unanimous but under its banner the entire hill districts carried out the rally any which way. Which perhaps explains why the violence became Kuki Vs Meitei. The naga representatives made it clear that ATSUM did not have the vote from the naga representatives. Another case of communalism started here, dragging the entire organization and its influence to bolster what is perceived to be the 'rightful demand' unilaterally decided by the few executives at the helm, effectively creating the hills vs valley protest. Perhaps, this is why the tires were set on fire near the gate to indicate a 'no-cross line,' a warning. This contest will drag on even late into the violence involving the 'Thang Ching' hills too. A deathly contest of boundary they have decided for themselves to be the line between the hill and valley.

This brings us to the next level of divide the 'psychology.' The tribal and non-tribal binary as we can see is already deeply communalized at the school and university level, this in turn creates a psychological divide. The geographical divide has been imposed by the CSOs themselves at the outbreak of the violence or perhaps before. The violence will become a vortex of anti-social elements, which will include youths that will arm themselves, the societies that will be dragged into the violence and become communalized, and then the armed groups of each society or tribe. Other groups will co-opt and join these ranks. Themselves, organizing into some sort of a reformation, an umbrella, strengthening the organizations and making them a monumental challenge to the government.

To me however, it was Manipuris fighting against Manipuris.

It doesn't make sense.

In the Eye of the Storm

It's like standing in the middle, encircled by the moments;

> *The screams,*
> *The cries,*
> *The flight,*
> *The pain,*
> *The fear,*
> *The pleas,*
> *The futility,*
> *The cutting,*
> *The prayers,*
> *The resignation,*
> *The tears,*
> *The heartburn,*
> *The rage,*
> *The mangling,*
> *The emotions,*
> *The anger,*
> *The helplessness,*
> *The sinking.*
> *The blood,*
> *The battering,*

How these sensations, they keep circling on and on, and on. They never stop, it keeps coming in waves, over and over. Restless and demanding, intense and relentless;

Like a storm.

These memories too, they refuse, and want to wail and wail;

And wail.

A tormenting storm, a behemoth that will keep circling round and round and;

Round.

GO TO THE CAMP

There was an old lady, I think her family abandoned her to her fate, while fleeing for their own life. It was clearly impossible to make a run with her. She was already very old. Something very odd took place. In the midst of the violence, young boys hurriedly carried her away and hid her.

Late evening the other day, when it was almost dark only for the flames from afar dimly lit, the commotions were growing louder and louder. I saw a Meitei lady *pleading* a couple on a scooter, to go to the military camp quickly. When they saw me, they started and left in a hurry.

There was no power. The road leading to *Game Village* was fiery red and yellow it lit up the night sky. You could hear thuds from explosions with sudden flashes. The place I was in, the *Langol hills*, engulfed in flames. They say it was the most affected part in Imphal. Naturally, they preferred the vicinity of the hills. Some weeks later, I returned from Chandel, I could see charred remains. There was a lot of burnt vehicles lining the roads on either side. The place still reeked of violence; it was only starting. The silent truth, to save, there was no;

Hero.

You either survive or die. That was the ultimate truth. I told to myself;

Manipur.

Population exchanges took place. We went back to Chandel. Then we heard about the disappearance. The killings, the gunfights, the stories from the relief camps, the deplorable condition. The deaths, the number they kept increasing. The killings, they became more and more gruesome. It was a contest of brutality.

To me it mirrored its past.

Slowly and slowly the foothills became the site of violence. The divide was taking shape.

Here's How History Is Repeating

The first insurgency in these bloodied lands is the *Manipuri Kuki Insurgency of 1917-1919*. It is the first sustained aggression against the authorities. By this I am not favoring one over the other, or sympathizing with the Kukis, I intend to keep the records straight. The insurgency started with the Kukis and in the later years gained momentum and included the nagas (especially Kamjong - the place is also home to Kukis even now) and Meiteis. The arms and ammunitions came from the 1891 ill-fated revolt, where many of it went, due to the disarmament orders imposed (Thang ta academies can better describe this event); it went to the hills and this became the tools for future revolts. Others learning how to devise their ammunitions, the pumpi for example; a tribal attempt at canon making.

The British had an unspoken policy of educating the princes Indians of noble birth or importance to teach them English culture and English taste but Indian by blood. This is evident even in the studies of India's history. By that the young royals, Churachand and even Bodhchandra were trained in this fashion. Although the royal had the dynastic eleven-gun salute, he was not eligible for the Chamber of princes. This should explain the matter of suzerainty and tributary. And the many expeditions carried out of Manipur like as if she was chained by the neck.

The Merger - The *'constitutional monarch'* by law even if he signs any document is null and void without the *'council of ministers'*. With this, we should be aware, the king has no power, the power was with the people even then. The merger agreement by all accounts is 'Invalid' - Manipur State Constitution Act 1947. There are varying accounts, and one indicates the monarch was willing due to the work of the certain political parties (irrespective they just wanted to be important) but he was not willing according to the terms of the agreement resulting in his house-arrest. Even when he wanted to go back to discuss the terms he was denied, as is proof in the telegrams. Otherwise, this would have been discussed in the Durbar nor would he have left Imphal abruptly leaving all even the Kuki loyalist who came with whatever arms they could find - only to safeguard Manipur.

THE BIRTH OF ASSAM RIFLES

The expansion of the British Raj in the hills. At this time Raja Gambhir Singh takes refuge at Sylhet. 1824-26, the *Sylhet Light Infantry* will play a vital role in the Anglo Burmese War. The first evidence of British Intervention in native politics. Given its proficiency, it will be revamped and will become the; *Cachar Levy*. The men recruited will compose of Punjabis, Gorkhali and the likes, much like modern day Assam Rifles. They will be used along with other forces like Manipur Levy and regular British forces, in the subjugation of;

1. Naga Hills.
2. Lushai Hills.
3. Khasi Hills.
4. The Plains of Burma
5. The Plains of Cachar.

Much like in modern day, Northeastern states. Akin to Chanakya's Artha shastra, perhaps this is the counter insurgency (COIN) model operations till date, it's palpably felt. And very likely, it hasn't change.

There are questions surrounding the *'Tipaimukh Rumor'*. If we are unsure of what is happening, perhaps an evaluation of the events surrounding our lives daily. If we are divided. Perhaps, if we feel exploited, given what we are experiencing. The question is what happens to us, the common people, with no fault of our own, trying to so hard to live, everyday trying to somehow make it through the day. Our roads and markets lined with 'mothers' with the little vegetables they have, to sell to make a living – all on their own, battling hunger and the bigger; battling life. A deplorable existence many Manipuris share, both hill and valley. Yet, we partake in the nightmare unfolding.

Sajik Tampak - The place is perhaps where the seed of this violence sprouted from the soil years before the SoO (Suspension of operations) even. The model eerily similar, to the 'Salwa Judum' movement in Chattisgarh. We feel contained in an environment. The pattern we see in Manipur eerily similar. How it started with the Tipaimukh rumor, demonizing us, manipulating sentiments. About Sajik Tampak and Tipaimukh, it is the ethnicity, and how we are now a fractured society.

'Bad Harvest — it felt as though the place was cursed. It came to a point that the elders of Sajik Tampak had to abandon their Christian faith and seek the guidance

of an — "Athimnu". She would read the signs and ask to seek the true reconciliation with the land.'

And indeed some 'Zou' elders arrived at Chandel. How did it pass through so many hands — It appears as though the land is 'weeping & searching' for the rightful master. Her hills — appear as though she 'wears her best' and readies herself everyday like a bride for her wedding, always at her best —, still full of hope — to be united. This tiny fertile haven, soaking and soaking in blood. How many times now, it is a 'wonder.'

Lister and Sylhet Infantry

With the advance of Burmese up to Manipur and finally to Cachar, the security of the British district, Sylhet was threatened. The authorities of Fort William became aware of the situation, Gobinda Chandra the deposed ruler of Cachar and Gambhir Singh took refuge in Sylhet. Edward Gait writes:

> "The defence the Surma valley was entrusted to a force called the Sylhet Local Battalion, afterwards the Sylhet Light Infantry, with headquarters at Sylhet. It was raised in 1824, and was recruited chiefly from Manipuris who had left their own country and settled in Sylhet and Cachar during the internal troubles and frequent Burmese invasions of the first quarters of the last century. Two companies of this regiment were stationed at Silchar, and at a later date it also occupied Cherrapunji."[21]

SHRI IRABOT SINGHA GI JAWAB.

This exchange is part of the fallout between Irabot and Nikhil Manipuri Mahasabha, July 20, 1946. Calcutta police had intercepted a memo from the president of NMM demanding that Irabot explain his attitude to the CPI to the NMM working committee. The Mahasabha itself, the memo declared, 'sympathizes with the aims of the Indian National Congress and is anti-communist'.

- John and Saroj Parratt. The page is from Bhagyavati Patrika.

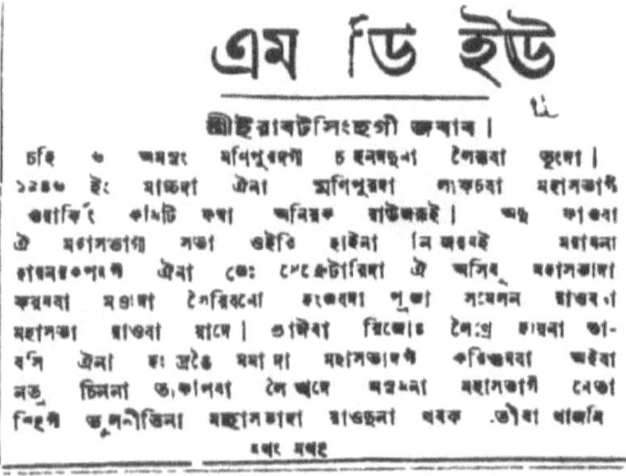

In the many pages I've read, there was the sense of betrayal he may have faced. Ultimately exiled into Burma. There, it appears he gathered fellow comrades and was going to enter Manipur. But for reasons best known, they say he suddenly fell ill and before he could reach Manipur. He became history. There are speculations, but I shall refrain from writing it and enforcing the narrative.

- and so be it.

Bhubon hills.

It is one of the abodes of Rongmei Indigenous religion. Going back to Nara Singh. The hills probably had something to do with Chandrapur (Jiribam). What was, the site from where the King prepared for the *liberation* of Manipur. This will ultimately culminate in the ill-fated treaty of *Jiribam 1833*. Where the fertile plains of Chandrapur will go to the British and Manipur will be left with a barren stretch of a land strip, what is present day;

Jiribam.

Akhui, 2022

The Radio Operator

This in relation to the *Naga Movement*, but in here; there is this particular house that will see three Manipuri generations.

The nagas who had some semblances of English education were recruited in the service of the British Raj. The highest rank a British Indian Subject, a "sepoy" could attain was that of a Subedar. Thanks to the "English" education - A particular naga from Chandel became a radio operator and was posted at Karachi. On his way home, sick and tired he stopped at a house 10 miles or so south of Tamenglong town - the biggest agglomeration of the Manipuri Kapuii Naga villages, better understood as "Khunjau" in Manipuri Meitei. Nestled high above the ridges overlooking the Barak (see the retreat on the map), The "Kameis" sheltered him for a week and nursed him back to health. The story goes - as a token of gratitude he left them a dinner set of fine China, the ones with floral prints in turquoise and pink. He would go on to become one, whose name among the 7 will be repeated in the course of history in the region. The start of the Naga insurgency - the NNC and its later more recognized proliferation into the armed struggle, the NSCN.

A few decades ago, the "same house" sheltered another person whose name, by virtue of his position, is at the center of Manipur Violence. I think it is safe to assume that civil contractors enter politics in their later life in Manipur, it is sort of like a rite of passage. I'm not entirely sure what was the work but he too stayed for weeks, then he went on to become the head of the state. And like the naga man, his name is bound to be remembered in Manipuri history, a contentious history at that, marred with gore and burning towns and villages, the likes never before witnessed in the history of Independent India.

And so, like the past repeating, I too took shelter,
ailing health; and receiving the same kindness. But
not in the same house, the younger brother's next to
it. Three generations later, if we look at relations –
although, it is as distant as the star.

Akhui, the retreat.

Only if it was; "Moirang"
A new one. Surely, it is Moirang. Be it Samlong, or the
restless hearts of the 44.
Or the start of the Meitei amalgamation. It must
dawn. Perhaps it will.

-

THE MIRAGE OF MOIRANG

Moirang where is your courage,
Did we lose it in the begging bowl of water.

Thingkhangphai why is your soil red,
Is it because of the fluttering flag.

Khongjom where is your bravery,
Did we entomb it in coppery glory.

Chassad where is your promise,
Did we abandon them in the hills.

Shangshak where is your ferocity,
Did we leave the sacrifice in history.

Kambiron where is your spark,
Is it lost with the eagle and the kite.

Another mirage of Moirang.

Letters from Burma and Manipur

I'll walk barefoot so I can talk with the soil. I'll immerse myself in the many rivers of Manipur. And tell the murky waters what happened here. So, our rivers, like *Imphal* and *Chakpi* can carry the stories. Tell the trees, tell the flowers, tell the stones, tell the bamboos, the names of the people, one by one, with devotion, love and care. As *Ningthee* (Chindwin) or *Ayerwaddy* do for Burma. On their way to the open seas and ocean, let the rivers fill them with our stories. And weep and weep, till the gods themselves, can no longer ignore us. And turn to our prayers, *just once even*. Then maybe, there will be divine intervention and healing, that our red-red land so desperately needs. Be it Burma, or the crescent highlands, our *homeland*.

If we must, perhaps our *Christian* brothers must double the prayers each day, or our *Pangal* brothers must read the Quran more diligently. Or perhaps, I must worship the gods, deities and spirits with utmost devotion in the temples and the little shrines. Perhaps, like Burma, we must make 'Bagan-like' *Pagoda Gardens*, to atone for the sins we've committed, unknowingly.

We are innocent. *Is Manipur not innocent?* My thoughts, they tell me: *'we'* are.

Call me Burma

Wrap me in the gardens of Bagan,
Call me Burma, call me Burma,
The Arakan Buddha watch with sorrow,
How my tears erupt from the tainted grounds,
How Mingun crumbles with heartache,
How Mogok Hills now bleed blood rubies,
And the Shan hills now bloom poison.

Wrap me in the gardens of Bagan,
Call me Burma, call me Burma,
Let me bloom into the most beautiful Padauk,
Let my spires pierce the sky's heart,
And cry to the Gods and cry to the Gods,
Let Ayerwaddy and Chindwin flow with tears,
Fill the oceans and the seas with my stories.

Wrap me in the gardens of Bagan,
Call me Burma, call me Burma,
Let the souls and spirits fly to the heavens,
Let their tears fall from the sky,
And soak the grounds and water the Pagodas.

Wrap me in the gardens of Bagan,
Call me Burma, call me Burma.

~*~

The Burst of

Butterflies

(Post-conflict Manipur)

This section is a work of *fiction*. An emotional exploration of life in Manipur, intended to provide insight into the psychological, social, and existential struggles faced by individuals in conflict. It does not glorify, justify, or promote violence, or any unlawful activity.

The narrative is crafted to encourage understanding, reflection, and critical thought on the complexities of war, identity, cost and human suffering. Any resemblance to real persons, events, or groups is purely coincidental unless explicitly stated.

Readers are encouraged to interpret this work through a humanitarian and empathetic lens, recognizing the nuanced realities of conflict and its impact on individuals and thereby societies.

BUTTERFLY STORY 1

I don't know how to even begin telling you, my story.
Sometimes I fail to understand why others won't see
the way I see things. I don't know if they think it is fun
to keep running from the law, not knowing when and
who will hit you. I want to tell them, I was like them
too, schools and college and now have a degree that
does not get me anything. I want to tell them I have
tried all that they will try too. Perhaps then they will
realize it is all but useless. It's funny how I can see
they will put all their effort in studies talking big
about subjects they will never use in their life in
Manipur. It is sad but that is the truth in most cases.
But I know like me all that books and knowledge is
going to end up under the bed in a metal box.

About me. I'm not from Imphal, my school life wasn't
that great, it was cycles on those roads they call 'a
road' but really, it generates a lot of money. There
was an odd one or two girls I liked, but I know them
very well, they must have liked so many other boys in
different *different* classes. I wonder how's mum right
now, I haven't seen her in a while. The last time I
came home she didn't seem very happy. And like
every time she kept asking me in a crying like manner
going about her work, from room to room then out
the house then in. It puts you in quite the pressure
really. She isn't crying though just the way she is and

how she tells her *'Problems'*; she'd ask if I plan to leave her alone too, then fuss about it more and then curse her fate and talk about the unending problem she has with our neighboring aunty. I've even started to hate her actually.

Just, from hearing mum tell me about all the things she would do to her. Nothing big but annoying petty little things. And her cat too, always stealing from our kitchen. And that cat is also so old, I wonder why how old is the cat now, it's not dying yet. It is still alive. A pure menace at night too. Why does anyone keep such a pet anyway. I don't even like the color of that cat. It's nearly all white except for the ugly orange patches that looks like as if it someone spat on it.

I had plans too, get a job like everyone else. Mum would have been happy and life would have been different too. In fact, very normal. But here we are talking about the other life.

Quite tiring to be honest. But there are many stories I will tell you that will make you think. I also did try hard very hard so hard and I couldn't anymore. Perhaps I wasn't meant to be. Or maybe I did it wrong I'll never know. And mum is not getting any younger too. There have been times we went hungry, then other times, that made us really sad and cry. Perhaps she knew I was crying too in my room but I didn't make a sound like mum. And I knew she was crying too.

Life was okay when dad was around. It all started after he left us. We didn't just finish our little savings, but ended up with debts hoping to get him back to health. Yet we borrowed and spent and still couldn't save him anyway. My dad, his temper was crazy. Don't tell anyone I told you this. But, that's how it was.

You know, there was this moment months after my father's death, we were in in such debt and mum had to go to Imphal and she had no money and no one would lend her any money, they knew that she wouldn't be able to pay them back anytime soon. She called whoever she knew on the phone one after the other hoping someone would help but no. So, she gave up and stared blankly into the room. I must be seventeen then, I didn't have anything with me but I felt I needed to do something about it so I told mum not to worry and that ill get some money from my friends for her fare. I walked to my friends and asked them whatever money they could help me with, shamelessly. Even if it was ten or fifty or hundred. And I got the same treatment like mum anyway. All except for this one friend who gave me five thousand. The paying back is another one altogether I will take years before I could finally pay him back.

Let's call it;

The Burst of Butterflies.

Let us try and make it pretty. Let's imagine you're around while I tell you the story and also tell you about everything and everything about it too. I was supposed to go out this afternoon. I didn't anyway. You cannot go beyond Imphal. Let's just say I don't know what is happening anymore. It was two years ago that the *violence* happened here. It was madness.

It is pretty much obvious. But do you feel it too? You feel abandoned?

Hmm, I do actually.

Guess my age (*forces a smile and pretends innocent forcing his eyes shut*).

Butterfly Story 2

'I'm telling you.
That place is never going to change.

I am telling you.
I feel sad but you know, leaving that place was a wise
decision.
Imagine if I was there now.
My god. It won't change. It won't change.'

'Yes, I think everyone there has gone crazy.'

'Look at their wives flaunting all that money meant
for the poor. While the entire state is burning.
They are heartless.
They are crazy.
Let them be you know. I don't care it's too much
now.'

'Hmmm...'

'I was talking about that her too you know and how
she lied.
I cannot believe it. She blocked me!
So, I told my friends about it, you know on video call.
 And that friend, that boy you remember?
I don't know when will he pick himself up.
But the place is anyway like that.
Nothing to do there, no hope.
You can't do anythi... .'

(His husband interrupts still poring at his book not looking up anyway)

'Start something like you maybe?'

'Haha.. Honey! (*sarcastically*). It's two years nothing has changed okay.

Nothing will work... it will not sell.
Only the poor people stay there now.
The rich, they all left.

Anyway.

On that video call. I told them very nicely.
Let them know too. So, I told them. Who is going to burn that cement gate anyway.

It won't burn even.'

(He flipped his hand looking straight at him. About to say something but stopped short. Turns back and continues going about the room and sizing and cleaning and folding and started the rant.)

'Yes. It won't burn also.
And it's right in the middle of the town.
Anybody who dares to do that will be dead already.
They won't be alive at all.
You know right? (rolls his eyes)

I told my friend in Manipur about our neighbor also.'

'Hmm you said that already.'

*(Turns back facing his husband, hands on his hips.
While his husband looked away from the book he was
reading and looking through his glass at him. He turns
back and moves to the other room and continues.
Talking louder this time.)*

'If you are not going for work tomorrow.
Maybe you should come over and help.

I have this big event coming up.
I cannot do it alone.
You can call your friends too.
Okay?'

(Shouts from the other room.)

'Yes!'

Butterfly Story 3

Is he asking me to speak. No not yet maybe. God, I shouldn't have accepted the call. I am tired of these live chats on TV. No one cares anyway. I wonder who is watching and even if they do are they really going to act on it. It's funny how he is speaking "geopolitics" and the army. That is surely going to go right over the head of the viewers.
Okay wait what is he saying – the governor? Good let him talk about it.
We really thought he would 'Harry Potter' wave his wand and fix everything in a jiffy. Arrest those lawbreakers and uphold the law. Yes! Say that say that. Good! Haha.
(Sips his tea)
Okay let me pretend to read the newspaper. I should look good on TV. Did he just say, all organizations should come together? Haha I might as well just laugh out loud. It will never happen. Say it. Say it. Yes.

'…… It will never happen. What are they talking about. It won't' (The voice of the other panelist ringing loud and clear.)

(Shakes his head and turns the newspaper) Oh wait I'm holding it upside down. Haha.. I hope the viewers didn't see it. Yes.. article 18, 19 and 21 yes.. say it say it.
Exactly, we cannot even move out of town. We cannot even go to the hill for the pilgrimage.

(Takes a long breathe) Okay, yes, the economy is completely destroyed. And we don't know how is anyone going to fix it.
Right, right, there is festivities going on in the middle of this crisis, yes. Must be the organizers, yes correct the organizers. Well in my opinion the ministers too. Good, I agree with you on that one. Everyone in Manipur should be given scheduled tribe status.
Right, no no.. the ones who don't want it can choose not to take it. Okay maybe I should add in. Let's do it.

'Sir so.. If I may add, yes a small one. (clears throat) I'm of the opinion, that those who do not wish to avail the benefits can simply choose not to take it. If an area so chooses not to take it, they can mention the family-name of that place say for example that family-name from Babupara can opt not to take it and the authorities can make a note of it. But they shouldn't oppose what others are asking from the Government.
That is all I have to add.
Thank you.'

(Sips his tea after delivering his opinion.)

Butterfly Story 4

She looked up the kitchen roof, the government
hasn't provided any help yet to their ward for the
roofing sheets damaged during the hailstorm last
year. She looked at the holes and grimaced as the
rains started. She could see the sky through the
kitchen roof. She stopped cutting the potatoes and
quickly went to grab a bucket to place below that
largest hole where water will pour down like water
from a hose.

'Abecha! Ho Abecha!
Get the other buckets and come inside!
It's about to rain.
Abecha! Abe… come come come.'

Abecha, comes in running with the bucket. Puts it
down and looks up the roof to check if she had
placed it properly.

'Go and get the tubs too.
Quickly girl.'

She moves out without saying a word. And comes
back with pots and tubs. Making noise around the
room as she places them one by one where she
thought it was needed but the roof had too many
holes.

'Get the rice to the other room.
Where is Bungo?'

*'He left for the relief camp to help with the water
distribution.'*

'That boy.
I mean why not let the others who can really help do
the work.
Your dad's still in the field?'

*'Yes. He hasn't returned.
Shall I take the plates too.?'*

'Yes girl, take the glasses too.
And listen.
Have they received the help from the government?'

*'I don't think so mama.
Even the family whose daughter in law killed herself
few weeks ago.
They have not received anything from the
government yet.*

*They said they will receive the installments this time.
No one knows when.'*

'Okay, we should talk to the neighbors I see.
Go now girl.
And cover the rice with the plates.'

'Okay.'

Leima has been trying to get government help for the
roofs but she thinks it is pointless now. It is not going
to come. During the floods that happened twice. Half
the walls of the kitchen got washed since the house
was the traditional wattle and daub. They managed

the washed sections with old plyboards and before
the rain became too heavy. She quickly took an
umbrella
And continued with her cooking. Staring bankly,
working the cooking, lost and feeling her emotions
well up inside her chest. She thought to herself.

- How long...

(Pattering noises start drowning everything.)

Butterfly Story 5

'Please, I swear I'll return it in two weeks' time.
You know me!'

Kantaraj gulped down a glass of it. The drinks at this
local brewery are strong. He feels disoriented but he
is determined to get some help from his friend. He
feels shameless but he feels helpless. Back in his
mind, the look of his unhappy wife keeps flashing in
and out & in and out. It breaks his heart. He's had
numerous arguments with her on almost everything
but he realizes it is simply to do with being poor and
unable to take up any work during this violence. The
farthest you can travel is the periphery of the city and
really there is no more work to do. There simply is –
'nothing.'

'Look friend, I.. I ... I... know!
But you know what, let's order another bottle.
Maybe some meat to have with it.
Shall we get chicken? What would you like?'

'Yes.. let's get some of that beef meat.

He downs another glass. The drink is very strong and
he feels how is moving from that light buzz to
something quickly dis-orienting. But that is blissful.
He felt his worries lighten up. They don't seem to
matter anymore. He thought to himself – drinking is
necessary in order to avoid going mental. While
feeling that slow slip, Tomba shakes his shoulder
gently, while both are visibly very drunk with their
heads slightly down but constantly chewing or talking

or drinking nonetheless.
Tomba can see Kantaraj knitting his brows and then
keeping a calm face and then knitting again. He
seemed to be trying to force uncomfortable thoughts
out of his mind. Despite not having much, he thought
he could lend him some.

That sound of payment on Google Pay chimed in.

'Tsk Tsk ...check!... Enjoy.'

Kantaraj looked up, his phone chimed. He almost
broke into tears. Tomba gives a dry smile slouched on
his chair.

~~~
~~~

This memoir

Beloved home, Manipur.

The many places, the valleys, the lakes, the names in the book – to me they appear deeply intertwined with the history, struggles, pain and memory of this battered land.

For the Manipuri, they only need to look in the mirror. And confront, the truth, their appearance, their nature, their history, their color, and their own;

Self.

~*~

Liberty

~*~

FURTHER READINGS

1. Political Development in Manipur 1919-1949, S M A W Chishti.
2. Cheitharol Kumpaba, Saroj Nalini Parrat.
3. The-North-east-Frontier-Of-India - Alexander Mckenzie
4. The-Meitheis - TC Hodgson
5. Manipur's breakdown and Mizorams Order - Development Studies, Mohammad Sajjad Hassan.
6. Historical account of the Nativist of Manipur and hill territory under its rule 1873
7. History of the Relations of the Government with the Hill Tribes of the North East Frontier of Bengal
8. Shan state Part 1 volume 1
9. 1944 Hill Peoples of Burma by Stevenson s
10. The Anals of Manipur - Rajendra Singh
11. The chin hills – Bertram S Carey
12. The lushai hills - Grace R Lewis
13. Tripuri Rajamala
14. Zo History – Vumson Suantak
15. The Lushai Expedition 1871 1872 – Robert Woodthorpe
16. The Anglo Kuki War 1917 1919 A Frontier Uprising – Jangkhomang Guite & Thongkholal Haokip
17. The Meitei (Kathe) Crown Service groups in Myanmar from the earliest times to the end of Monarchical Rule, Dr. Nwe Ni Hlaing.
18. Hijam Irabot and the Radical Socialist Democratic Movement in Manipur – John & Saroj Arambam Parrat.
19. The London Gazette, AUGUST 14, 1891.
20. Irawat sentinel of the east – Tikendra, Salam, Santa, RK Sanajaoba.
21. Manipur State Constitution Actt, 1947
22. History of the people of Manipur, Hareshwar Goswami.
23. The Lushai Hills, Robert Reid
24. Frontier Officers in Colonial NE India – Suhash Chatterjee (Colonel Lister).
25. Hijam Irabot and Political Developments in Manipur – Karam Manimohan Singh.
26. Anal Customary Laws and its Practices - Dr. B.D. Thumdal Anal
27. Anal Naga (Pakan) Tribe. Identity, Culture and Political Administration – Onhring Langhu
28. Pot Internment System, Hansa Mehta Library. AK Sharma.

29. The historical account of Kabaw Valley – RK Maheshsana, The Sangai Express
30. Jayantia Rajamala.
31. HRA sets record straight, rubbishes allegations – Epao.net
32. 1929 Notes on the Thadou Kukis. Shaw.

www.ingramcontent.com/pod-product-compliance
Lightning Source LLC
Chambersburg PA
CBHW062219150726
47991CB00006B/2350